ALLELUIA!
AMEN!

ALLELUIA! AMEN!

MUSIC FOR THE LITURGY
Edited by Margaret Daly

Director of Music at
The Irish Institute of Pastoral Liturgy

veritas

VERITAS

VERITAS PUBLICATIONS
7 & 8 Lower Abbey Street, Dublin 1
First published 1978

ACKNOWLEDGEMENTS

The Publishers are grateful to the following for permission to use copyright material:
Sr Lucia Fay *for Let All Who Are Baptised, Bring Us Back To You, O Lord Our God, Christ Our Lord Has Come To Save His People;* Fr Paul Décha *for The Lourdes Magnificat, Bring Us Back To You O Lord Our God, Let All Who Are Baptised Walk In The Light Of Christ, Alleluia Ps. 112;* Sr Aideen O'Sullivan *for The Beatitudes, You Are My Servant, Surely He Has Borne Our Griefs, Steadfast Love, I Am The Way;* Michael Hodgetts *for Holy Mary Full Of Grace, The Lourdes Magnificat;* Karen Barrie & J. Chapman *for I Will Celebrate;* Mayhew McCrimmon Ltd. *for Love Is His Word, Jesus Took Bread;* Board of Gov. E.C. *for Gift Of Finest Wheat;* N.A.L.R. *for Our Help Is In The Name Of The Lord, Sing To The Lord, Deliver Us O God Of Israel;* A. P. Watt & Son *for Psalms 22 and 129;* R. Connolly *for Where There Is Charity And Love;* G. Chapman *for This Is My Will, Sinless Maiden;* Fr Joseph Walshe *for Like The Deer That Yearns, Christ Suffered For You;* Benedictine Found. of State of Vermont *for O With What Joy We Sing Of Mary, Unless A Man Is Born From Above, The Lord Jesus, Yahweh, Come To Me;* Clarence Rivers *for God Is Love;* Holub & Assoc. N.Y. *for God Is Love;* G.I.A. *for May Christ Live In Our Hearts, I Am The Bread Of Life;* The Word Of God Music *for The Light Of Christ;* Mary McCooey *for Jesus Christ Is Lord, Fill Me With Your Praise;* S.E.F.I.M. *for Let All Who Are Baptized, When The Time Came To Stretch Out His Arms, Renew Your Hearts, Alleluia Ps 112, Though So Many We Are One, Christ Our Lord Has Come To Save His People, Hymn To Love, Let Us Welcome The Lord, Spring Of New Hope, Glory Be To You, Arise Jerusalem, Christ Is Our Lord, Song Of The Banquet, Alleluia Ps 148, Lumen Christi, Holy Mary Full Of Grace, Lourdes Magnificat, I Search Everywhere;* David Higham Assoc. Ltd. *for Morning Has Broken;* Colin Mawby *for How Can I Repay The Lord;* David Austin *for Day By Day;* F.E.L. *for Hear O Lord, All Of My Life;* World Library Publications Inc. *for Heavens Drop Dew From Above, Maranatha, Let Me Sing Of Your Law, I Want To Sing, Psalm 150, Priestly People, Grant To Us Lord, You Are The Honour, Yes I Shall Arise, Without Seeing You, Give Praise To The Lord All You Men, All The Earth Proclaim The Lord, Keep In Mind, All You Nations, My Soul Is Longing For Your Peace;* Fiontán Ó Cearbhaill *for Sé An Tiarna M'aoire;* Seán óg Ó Tuama *for Caomhnaigh Mé A Thiarna;* ICEL *for Music For The Eucharist;* Fr Thomas Egan *for The Lord Is My Shepherd;* Fr Kevin Healy OSB *for Molaigí An Tiarna, Alleluia;* Sr Pamela Stotter *for texts of Christ Is Alive, Song Of Banquet, Arise Jerusalem, Christ Is Our Lord, Spring Of New Hope, Let Us Welcome The Lord, Hymn To Love.*

Designed by Liam Miller
Cover by Steven Hope
ISBN 905092 47 3
Printed and bound in the Republic of Ireland by
Cahill Printers, Dublin

CONTENTS

BISHOP DERMOT O'MAHONY

AUXILIARY BISHOP OF DUBLIN

Margaret Daly and the Irish Institute of Pastoral Liturgy are to be warmly commended for producing this new liturgical hymnal. It contains not only a selection of hymns, but also music for the parts of the Mass. The hymns are arranged according to the structure of the Liturgy, with Entrance Hymns, Offertory Hymns, Communion Hymns etc, and a very valuable addition is the grouping of hymns for the different sacraments.

However, it is perhaps the presentation of this hymnal which makes it a significant step forward in the renewal of liturgical music in Ireland. Not only are the priorities for music in the Liturgy clearly indicated, but the notes which accompany each section provide the priest, the organist and the congregation with a kind of "teach yourself" kit for understanding the role of music and song and its appropriate application to any specific celebration.

Needless to say there are many hymns in this book which could very happily be used also in para-liturgical celebrations, or in prayer groups.

I wish the hymnal and the work of the Irish Institute of Pastoral Liturgy every success.

✠ DERMOT O'MAHONY,
Auxiliary Bishop of Dublin.

INTRODUCTION

"ALLELUIA" "AMEN". These two words are at the heart of the Eucharist, and thus at the centre of our lives as Christians.

"Alleluia!" "Praise the Lord!" This is our response to God's goodness; to creation; to our existence; to the plans God has for us; to the sending of Christ; to a "future full of hope" (*Jer 29:11*).

"Amen!" "It is true!" "May it become true in us!" – Our commitment to follow the way of life shown to us by Jesus; our decision to live no longer for ourselves but for him; our concern for our fellow pilgrims as we journey towards the Father.

In the celebration of the Eucharist, the Gospel Acclamation and the Great Amen are given fullness of expression when they are sung. Indeed, if we were to sing nothing else we would still be making effective use of music. "When we sing our 'Amen', we are signing our name" (Augustine), pledging to sing with our lives what we sing with our voices.

Through the Eucharist, we are empowered to live up to what we proclaim, "to love and serve the Lord". Our "Alleluia, Amen" becomes the song we sing along the road, to lighten our journey and unite us pilgrims in joy. "Sing," says Augustine, "and keep on walking."

This hymnal contains music drawn from Irish and international sources which is used at the Irish Institute of Pastoral Liturgy. It does not include the complete repertory of the Institute, but seeks to make available some recent compositions as a complement to the traditional hymnody, Irish language hymns, and Gregorian chant which are already available in publications such as *The Veritas Hymnal, Christian Burial*, and *Jubilate Deo*.

It is hoped that this book will help towards answering the need for a contemporary style of liturgical music, biblical in inspiration, reverent in quality, and acceptable to young and old alike. The responsorial method of singing, which is being rediscovered as an encouragement toward congregational singing, is given considerable stress. There is provision for the new opportunities for singing which occur in the revised rites of the sacraments. It is also hoped that this book may be a stepping stone toward the involvement of lay people in the official prayer of the Church. Liturgical notes are included so that church musicians who use the book may be encouraged to deepen their appreciation and understanding of their liturgical ministry.

The editor wishes to thank the following people who helped in the preparation of this work: Sr Mary Lucia, Sr Fintan Davis, Fr Jerry Threadgold, Fr Sean Swayne, Fr Frank O'Loughlin, Sr Pamela Stotter.

THE EUCHARIST

PRIORITIES IN SINGING

Priority should be given to the more important points.

1. Acclamations

(Gospel Acclamation, Sanctus, Memorial Acclamation, Great Amen) "Happy the people who learn to acclaim you" *(Ps 88)*. The acclamation is a "festal shout", a strong affirmative expression of the congregation's acceptance and praise of God's word and action and of their commitment to the following of Christ. Acclamations should never be taken over by the choir to the exclusion of the congregation.

2. Dialogue Chants

(Chants at the Proclamation of the Gospel, Dialogue before the Preface, Concluding Rite, the third form of the Penitential Rite). Because the Eucharist is a communal action, the dialogues between priest and congregation are of special value. Theoretically, all the dialogues may be sung, and music is provided in the *Roman Missal*. However, following the principle that not all singable parts need be sung *(IGMR 19)*, we provide here only the more important dialogues.

3. Responsorial Psalm

Having pondered the word of God in their hearts, the people respond by singing the refrain of the psalm. To facilitate reflection on the Word, there may be a brief period of silence between the reading and the responsorial psalm. Responsorial psalms will be found in pages 35 to 62

INSTRUMENTAL MUSIC

Instrumental Music can be effective at certain moments in the eucharistic celebration:

– immediately after the Opening Prayer, to create an attitude of receptivity to the Word about to be proclaimed;

– after the Readings, to help the faithful "to ponder these things in their hearts" *(Lk 2:52)*;

– as a prelude to the Gospel Acclamation while incense is being placed in the thurible;

– at the preparation of the gifts (see page 16);

– after the *Agnus Dei* at a concelebrated Eucharist, if there is a delay while communion is being distributed to the concelebrants;

– during or after the communion procession;

– at the end of the liturgy.

9

MUSIC FOR THE INTRODUCTORY RITES

ENTRANCE SONG

The purposes of the entrance song are to open the celebration, help the people to be conscious of themselves as a worshipping community, introduce the liturgical season or feast, and accompany the procession. Sufficient time should be given to the entrance song if it is to achieve its purposes. Entrance songs for the liturgical seasons may be chosen from the list on pages 24 to 26. During ordinary time a song reflecting the theme of the entrance antiphon (*Roman Missal*), or some aspect of the readings of the day, may be chosen. On Sunday, the day of the resurrection, Easter songs are always appropriate.

Examples of Entrance Songs:

Alleluia *(Ps 1 12)*   42
All the earth   54
Christ is alive   76
Christ Our Lord, has come to save his people   81
Hear, O Lord   72
I will celebrate   35
Let all who are baptised   100
May Christ live in our hearts   95
Priestly people   64
Though so many, we are one   79
The light of Christ   117
Song of the Banquet   108
Glory be to you   112
Other may be chosen in accordance with the principles given above.

PENITENTIAL RITE

This is the people's cry for mercy. It may be dialogued by the priest or cantor with the congregation. It is good, on occasion, to use the ancient Greek *Kyrie Eleison*. This is a link with our past as well as with the Eastern Rite liturgies. The alternative invocations found in pages 392 to 395 of the *Roman Missal* may be adapted to the melodies given in settings A and B.

A

Roman Missal — Seóirse Bodley

P. Lord Jesus, you raise us to new life: Lord, have mer - cy.
C. Lord, have mer - cy.

P. Lord Jesus, you forgive us our sins: Christ, have mer - cy.
C. Christ, have mer - cy.

P. Lord Jesus, you feed us with your body and blood: Lord, have mer - cy.
C. Lord, have mer - cy.

B

Plainchant

Lord have mer - cy. Christ have mer - cy. Lord have mer - cy.

Alternative

Ky -ri - e e - le - i - son.
Christ - e e - le - i - son.
Ky -ri - e e - le - i - son.

C

Roman Missal

P. You were sent to heal the con - trite: Lord, have mer - cy.
C. Lord, have mer - cy.

P. You came to call sin - ners: Christ, have mer - cy.
C. Christ, have mer - cy.

P. You plead for us at the right hand of the Fa - ther; Lord, have mer - cy.
C. Lord, have mer - cy.

Alternative

ed. Vat. XVI

Ký -ri-e, e-lé - i-son. *ij.* Christe, e-lé -i-son. *ij.* Ký-ri-e, e-lé- i-son. Ký-ri-e, e-lé- i-son.

11

GLORIA

This ancient hymn of praise is used only on Sundays outside Advent and Lent, on solemnities and feasts, and at solemn local celebrations. It is sung by the congregation, by the people alternatively with the choir, or by the choir alone. The *Gloria* provides an opportunity for the choir to sing a setting from the Gregorian or polyphonic repertory.

Seóirse Bodley

Glo - ry to God in the high - est, and peace to his peo - ple on earth.

Lord God, hea - ven-ly King,_ Al - migh - ty_ God and_ Fa - ther, we wor - ship_

you, we give you_ thanks, we praise you_ for your_ glo - ry. Lord

Je - sus_ Christ, on -ly Son of the Fa - ther, Lord God, Lamb of God, you

take a - way the_ sin_ of the world, have mer - cy on us. You are

sea - ted at the right hand of the Fa - ther, re - ceive our_ prayer. For

you a - lone are the Ho- ly One, You a - lone are the Lord.__

You a - lone are the Most High, Je - sus_ Christ, with the

Ho - ly_ Spi-rit in the glo - ry of God the_ Fa - ther. A - men.

Alternative version

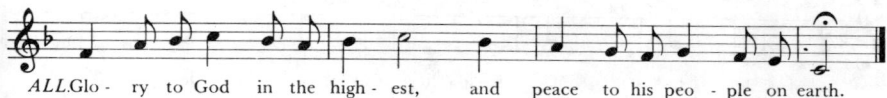

ALL.Glo - ry to God in the high - est, and peace to his peo - ple on earth.

CHOIR: Lord God, heavenly King,
Almighty God and Father,
we worship you, we give you thanks,
we praise you for your glory.

ALL: Glory to God in the highest,
and peace to his people on earth.

CHOIR: Lord Jesus Christ, only Son of the Father,
Lord God, Lamb of God,
You take away the sin of the world:
have mercy on us.

ALL: Glory to God in the highest,
and peace to his people on earth.

CHOIR: You are seated at the right hand of the Father:
receive our prayer.

ALL: Glory to God in the highest,
and peace to his people on earth.

CHOIR: For you alone are the Holy One,
You alone are the Lord,
You alone are the Most High,
Jesus Christ,
with the Holy Spirit,
in the Glory of God the Father.

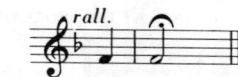

ALL: A - men

MUSIC FOR THE LITURGY OF THE WORD

RESPONSORIAL PSALM

When the scriptures are read in the church Christ himself is speaking to us. The people respond to God's message in words given by God himself, the psalms. The verses are sung from the ambo by a cantor. It is helpful if he sings the refrain first, inviting the congregation to repeat it once, before he begins the psalm verse. If music for the psalm of the day is not available, another suitable psalm, having some bearing on the reading that precedes it, may be chosen. Responsorial psalms are listed on page 128 and will be found in pages 35 to 62.

GOSPEL ACCLAMATION

The proclamation of the gospel is the climax of the liturgy of the Word. The introductory rites, first reading, and psalm, have all been by way of preparation for this moment. The people stand and acclaim the presence of Christ in his word by singing "Alleluia" (or its alternative during Lent). Of its nature, this acclamation requires to be sung. If it is not sung, it may be omitted (IGMR 39).

DIALOGUE CHANTS BEFORE AND AFTER THE GOSPEL

Singing here helps to sustain the atmosphere of expectancy and praise created by the singing of the Gospel Acclamation, and it lends a dignified surround to the proclamation of the gospel.

13

A

Al - le - lu - ia, Al - le - lu - ia. Al - le - lu - ia.

Verse sung by cantor

'I am the good shepherd' says the Lord. I know my own sheep and my own know me.

GOSPEL ACCLAMATION (During Lent)

Glo - ry to you, O Christ, you are the Word of — God.

CHANTS AT THE PROCLAMATION OF THE GOSPEL

C. The Lord be with you. P. And al - so with you.

C. A reading from the Holy Gospel according to — P. Glo - ry to you, Lord.

C. This is the gospel of the Lord. P. Praise to you, Lord Je - sus Christ.

B

GOSPEL ACCLAMATION Paul Décha

ALL; Al - le - lu - ia, Al - le - lu - ia, Al - le - lu - ia.

Verse sung by cantor

Harden not your hearts to - day, but listen to the voice of the Lord.

Other Gospel Acclamations chosen from the lectionary may be sung to this melody.

GOSPEL ACCLAMATION (During Lent) Robert J. Batastini

Praise and ho - nour to you, Lord Je - sus Christ.

14

CHANTS AT THE PROCLAMATION OF THE GOSPEL   Roman Missal

C. The Lord be with you.   P. And al - so with you.

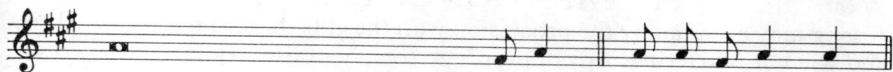

C. A reading from the Holy Gospel according to ... P. Glo - ry to you, Lord.

This is the gospel of the Lord. P. Praise to you, Lord Je - sus Christ.

C

GOSPEL ACCLAMATION

Al - le - lu - ia, Al - le - lu - ia, Al - le - lu - ia.

Verse sung by cantor

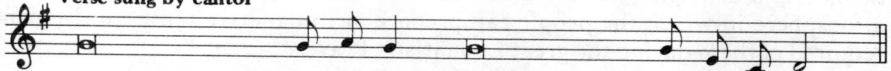

Speak, Lord, your servant is listen-ing, You have the message of e - ter - nal life.

Other Gospel acclamations chosen from the
lectionary may be sung to this melody.

GOSPEL ACCLAMATION (During Lent)   Traditional

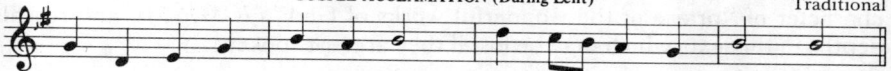

Praise to you Lord Je - sus Christ, King of e - ter - nal glo - ry.

CHANTS AT THE PROCLAMATION OF THE GOSPEL   Roman Missal

P. The Lord be with you.   C. And al - so with you.

A reading from the holy Gospel accor - ding to ... C. Glo - ry to you, Lord.

P. This is the Gospel of the Lord. C. Praise to you, Lord Je - sus Christ.

15

MUSIC FOR THE LITURGY
OF THE EUCHARIST

PREPARATION OF THE GIFTS

A song may accompany the procession with the gifts. It need not speak of bread and wine or of offering. Any appropriate song of praise, rejoicing, thanks, etc., in keeping with the season may be used, e.g.:

Bring bread   98
How can I repay the Lord   40
Hear, O Lord   72
Christ is alive   76
The Beatitudes   69
All of my life   71
Priestly people   64
All you nations   51
All the earth   54
Molaigí an Tiarna   50

Other appropriate songs may be chosen according to the principles given above.

Singing by the people during the preparation of the gifts is not always desirable. Silence, choral singing, or instrumental music can often create a relatively calm atmosphere in which the people can prepare for the more intense involvement required of them during the great Eucharistic Prayer.

THE EUCHARISTIC PRAYER

This is the centre and high point of the entire celebration. Music brings out its character of "praise of the wonderful works of God" (*IGMR 54*), and reveals depths in the texts which may be lost if they are just spoken.

DIALOGUE BEFORE THE PREFACE

Here, the change to a standing posture and the singing emphasise that a new and important part of the celebration is now beginning. The priest invites the people to lift up their hearts as he praises God on their behalf. On three occasions the people intervene with their acclamations:

SANCTUS

A resounding hymn of praise in which the Church on earth joins in the joyful song of the heavenly liturgy;

MEMORIAL ACCLAMATION

The priest invites the people to proclaim the mystery of faith. Music adds a dimension of affirmation to this proclamation of the central Christian belief;

GREAT AMEN

The people make the praise of the Eucharistic Prayer their own. They commit themselves to the living out of the death and resurrection of Christ.

A

Roman Missal

P. The Lord be with you. C. And al - so with you. P. Lift up your hearts.

C. We lift them up to the Lord. P. Let us give thanks to the

Lord our God. C. It is right to give him thanks and praise.

SANCTUS

Seóirse Bodley

Ho - ly Ho - ly, Ho - ly Lord, God of pow'r and might. Hea - ven and

earth are full of your glo - ry. Ho - san - na in the high - est. Bles - sed is

he who comes in the name of the Lord. Ho - san - na in the high - est.

MEMORIAL ACCLAMATION

Seóirse Bodley

Dy - ing you de - stroyed our death, ri - sing

you re - stored our life, Lord Je - sus, come in glo - ry.

GREAT AMEN

Seóirse Bodley

A - men, A - men, A - men, A - men.

17

B

Roman Missal

P. The Lord be with you.

C. And al - so with you.

P. Lift — up — your hearts.

C. We lift — them up to the Lord.

P. Let us give thanks to the Lord our God. C. It is right to give him thanks and praise. —

SANCTUS

Douglas Mews

Ho - ly, ho - ly, ho - ly Lord, God of power and might

Hea - ven and earth are full of your glo - ry. Ho - san - na in the high - est.

Bless- ed is he who comes in the name of the Lord. Ho - san- na in the high - est.

MEMORIAL ACCLAMATION

Gaelic

When we eat this bread and — drink this cup, we pro - claim your death, Lord —

Je - sus, un - til you come in glo - ry, un - til you come in glo - ry.

GREAT AMEN

Fintan O' Carroll

A - men, A - men, A - men.

18

C Roman Missal

P. The Lord be with you. C. And al - so with you.

P. Lift up your hearts. C. We lift them up to the Lord.

P. Let us give thanks to the Lord our God. C. It is right to give him thanks and praise.

SANCTUS
Roman Missal

Ho - ly, ho - ly, ho - ly, Lord, God of power and might, hea - ven and earth are full of your glo - ry. Ho - san -na in the high - est. Bles-sed is he who comes in the name of the Lord Ho - san - na in the high - est.

SANCTUS

Sanctus, *Sanctus, Sanctus Dóminus De - us Sába- oth. Pleni sunt cæ-li et terra gló- ri-a tu - a. Hosánna in excélsis. Benedíctus qui ve-nit in nómi - ne Dómini. Ho-sanna in excélsis.

MEMORIAL ACCLAMATION
Roman Missal

Dy-ing you de-stroyed our death, ri-sing you re-stored our life. Lord Je - sus, come in glo - ry.

GREAT AMEN
Plainchant

A - men, A - men, A - men.

19

MUSIC FOR THE COMMUNION RITE

THE LORD'S PRAYER

This is the prayer of the whole community. It should not be monopolised by a soloist or choir. Adopting the principle that it is not always necessary to sing every singable text, it is better that all recite the Lord's Prayer than for a small group within the congregation to sing it. Unlike the acclamations, the Lord's Prayer does not of its nature require to be sung. If the doxology is sung, it is preferable for the priest to sing the prayer "Deliver us Lord from every evil . . ." (page [123], *Roman Missal*).

A

THE LORD'S PRAYER

Seóirse Bodley

Our— Fa - ther, who— art in— heav'n, hal - lowed be thy name;

Thy King - dom— come; Thy— will be done on — earth as it is in—

heav'n. Give— us this day our— dai - ly— bread; and for - give us— our—

tres - pas - ses as we for - give those who— tres - pass a - gainst us; and—

lead us not in - to temp - ta - tion, but de - li - ver us from— e - vil.

DOXOLOGY

For the king-dom, the— pow - er, and the glo - ry are— yours,— now and for - e - ver.

B

Adapted from chants
of the Byzantine liturgy

Our Fa-ther, who art in hea-ven hal-lowed be thy name, thy king-dom come,

thy will be done on earth as it is in hea-ven. Give us this day our dai-ly bread,

and for-give us our tres-pas-ses as we for-give those who tres-pass a-gainst us;

And lead us not in-to temp-ta-tion, but de-li-ver us from e - vil.

DOXOLOGY

For the king - dom the power and the glo - ry are yours, now and for - e - ver.

AGNUS DEI

This chant accompanies the breaking of bread and may be repeated as often as is necessary while the bread is being broken. It may be sung by all, or alternated between cantor, or choir, and the congregation. On occasion it may be sung by the choir with the people listening, especially where there is a possibility of using a setting from the Gregorian or polyphonic repertory.

A

AGNUS DEI

Seóirse Bodley

Lamb of God, you take a-way the sins of the world: have mer - cy on us.

rall.

Lamb of God you take a - way the sins of the world: grant us— peace.

21

B

Douglas Mews

Lamb of God, you take a-way the sins of the world have mer - cy on us

Lamb of God, you take a- way the sins of the world, grant us peace. ——

C

Plainchant

1-2.Lamb of God, you take a - way the sins of the world, have mer - cy on us.
3. Lamb of God, you take a - way the sins of the world —— grant us —— peace.

AGNUS DEI

A-gnus De- i, *qui tollis peccáta mundi:mi-se-ré-re no-bis. *ij.* Agnus De- i, *qui tollis peccáta

mundi: dona nobis pa-cem.

COMMUNION SONG

The communion song expresses the spiritual union of the communicants, shows the joy of all, and makes the communion procession an act of brotherhood. Suitable songs would refer to the liturgical season, the feast being celebrated, or to themes of joy, praise, and fraternity. The communion antiphon (*Roman Missal*) is a helpful guideline in the choice of the appropriate song. For practical reasons the responsorial method is most appropriate. The people can easily memorise a short refrain, in which case they will not need to carry hymn books in the procession.

Examples of communion songs are:
Gift of finest wheat   89
Without seeing you   67
Though so many, we are one   79
Gift of peace   76
I am the bread of life   70
Jesus took bread   42
Love is his word   114
This is my will   113
Christ is our lord   73
Hymn to love   111

The Lord is my shepherd   118
God is love   74
Where there is charity and love   93
Christ is alive   76
Other appropriate songs may be chosen according to the principles given above.

HYMN OR PSALM OF PRAISE AFTER COMMUNION

This may be appropriate if there has been no singing during the communion procession. It is to be distinguished in its function from the song during the communion procession. Some examples are:

When the time came   80
All of my life   71
Fill us with your praise   101
How can I repay the Lord   40
Sing a new song to the Lord   44
The Lourdes Magnificat   122
Other appropriate songs may be chosen in accordance with the principles given above.

MUSIC FOR THE CONCLUDING RITE

When the concluding rite is sung, the celebration ends on a note of praise and joy. "The people return to their daily lives of good works praising and blessing God" (IGMR 57).

CONCLUDING RITE   Roman Missal

P. The Lord   be with you.   C. And al - so with you.

Response to the Blessing   C. A - men.

Lucien Deiss

P. The mass is   en - ded, go__ in peace.   C. Thanks   be   to   God.

Alternative   Lucien Deiss

P. Go in peace   to love and serve__ the Lord.   C. Thanks   be   to   God.

23

THE LITURGICAL YEAR

In the course of the year the Church unfolds the whole mystery of Christ from the incarnation and nativity to the ascension, to Pentecost and the expectation of the blessed hope of the coming of the Lord. Thus recalling the mysteries of the redemption, she opens up to the faithful the riches of her Lord's powers and merits so that these are in some way made present for all time; the faithful lay hold of them and are filled with saving grace.

The Church honours the Blessed Mary, mother of God, with a special love. She is inseparably linked with her son's saving work, and is an image of what the Church desires and hopes to be *(Constitution on the Liturgy, 102–103)*. The following are some examples of appropriate songs for the various seasons of the liturgical year.

ADVENT

Steadfast love   87
The Lourdes Magnificat   122
For you shall go out in joy   104
Hear, O Lord   72
Hail Mary   103
Heavens, drop dew from above   66
Maranatha   63
Come, O Lord   92
Yahweh   94
You are the honour   68
Sinless maiden   102
O comfort my people   109
Arise Jerusalem   110
Spring of new hope   106
Let us welcome the Lord   105

Responsorial Psalms
Bring us back to you *(Ez 36)*   40
Grant to us, O Lord *(Jer 31)*   56
My soul is longing for your peace *(Ps 130)*   55
Show us, Lord, your mercy *(Ps 84)*   38

CHRISTMASTIDE

The light of Christ   117
Christ, Our Lord, has come to save his people   81
Priestly people (Verses 1 to 6)   64
Sing a new song to the Lord   44
Sinless maiden   102
Hail Mary   103
O with what joy   99
Christ is alive   76

24

Responsorial Psalms
Alleluia *(Ps 112)*   42
Alleluia *(Ps 150)*   54
Give praise to the Lord all you men *(Ps 112)*   52
Jesus Christ is Lord *(Ps 144)*   47
Alleluia *(Ps 148)*   59
Sing to the Lord, Alleluia *(Ps 95)*

PENTECOST

Come Holy Spirit   96
The Spirit of the Lord   94
You are my servant   85
May Christ live in our hearts   95
The Beatitudes (Refrain 1)   69
Prayer of St Francis   98
Priestly people   64

Responsorial Psalms
The Lord is my shepherd *(Ps 22)*   118
All you nations *(Ps 65)*   51
All the earth *(Ps 99)*   54
Jesus Christ is Lord *(Ps 144)*   47
Grant to us O lord *(Jer 31)*   56
Other songs may be chosen according to the principles given above.

MARY

You are the honour   68
Priestly people (Verses 1-2)   64
O with what joy   99
Hail Mary   103
The Lourdes Magnificat   122
Sinless maiden   102
Holy Mary full of grace   113
Spring of new hope   106

OTHER LITURGICAL OCCASIONS

BAPTISM

In the celebration of baptism the people of God, represented not only by the parents, godparents and relatives, but also as far as possible by friends, neighbours, and some members of the local Church, should take an active part (*Rite of Baptism; General Instruction, Par. 7*). By participating in song, the people show their common faith and their joy as the newly-baptised person is received into the community of the Church. The celebration deepens the faith of all present and helps them to grow in their appreciation of their own baptism. If the sacrament takes place during the Eucharist, the principles on page 9 apply.

There are several occasions for singing in the rite itself. The musical unity of the celebration may be enhanced when one song is used several times with appropriate verses chosen for each occasion. The following are examples of appropriate songs:

OPENING PSALM OR SONG

Come Holy Spirit   96
The Spirit of the Lord   94
Priestly people   64
All the earth   54
Grant to us, O Lord (Adult Baptism)   56
The light of Christ   117

SONG DURING PROCESSION TO THE AMBO

Show us, Lord, your mercy *(Ps 84)*   38
Lord, you have the words *(Ps 118)*   45
Let me sing of your law *(Ps 118)*   46
More verses of the hymn chosen from section 1

PSALM OR SONG
IN RESPONSE TO THE WORD OF GOD

Unless a man   78
The Lord is my shepherd *(Ps 22)*   118
S'é an Tiarna m'aoire *(Ps 22)*   49
I will celebrate *(Ps 88)*   35
Like the deer that yearns *(Ps 41-42)*   48
Have mercy, Lord *(Ps 50)* (Adult Baptism)   46

27

SONG DURING PROCESSION TO BAPTISTRY

The Lord is my shepherd *(Ps 22)* 118
Like the deer that yearns *(Ps 41-42)* 48
The Beatitudes (Refrain 1) 69
Any suitable hymns from sections 1 to 3.

ACCLAMATION AFTER THE BAPTISM

Priestly people (Refrain) 64
Let all who are baptised (Refrain) 100
Christ, Our Lord, has come to save his people (Refrain) 81
Alleluia *(Ps 112)* (Refrain) 42
I will celebrate *(Ps 88)* (Refrain) 35
Jesus Christ is Lord (Refrain) 47

ACCLAMATION DURING PROCESSION TO ALTAR

A refrain from the previous section
Though so many, we are one (Refrain) 79

CONCLUDING SONG

Any song of thanksgiving and Easter joy, e.g.:
The light of Christ 117
The Lourdes Magnificat 122
May Christ live in our hearts 95
Let all who are baptised 100
Christ, Our Lord, has come to save his people 81
Alleluia *(Ps 112)* 42
I will celebrate *(Ps 88)* 35
Jesus Christ is Lord *(Ps 114)* 47
Lumen Christi 114
Other songs may be chosen according to the principles given above.

CONFIRMATION

Those who have been baptised continue on the path of Christian initiation
through the sacrament of confirmation. They are called to be Christ's witnesses
before the world and are endowed by the Holy Spirit with special strength *(LG
2, 11)*. Ordinarily, confirmation takes place during the celebration of the
Eucharist. The principles on page 9 apply.

It may be helpful to introduce singing during the anointing once the formula
has been heard by the people. For appropriate songs and Responsorial Psalms,
see *Pentecost*, page 26.

PENANCE

In communal penance celebrations and penitential services the role of the community in the forgiveness of sin emerges more clearly. Within the solidarity of a worshipping community we hear God's word, we acknowledge our sinfulness, we experience God's forgiveness and proclaim his praise. The following are some examples of appropriate songs:

OPENING SONG

Come to me   97
Yes, I shall arise   50
Grant to us, O Lord   56
Hear, O Lord (Verse 3)   72
Renew your hearts   77
Bring us back to you   40
Christ suffered for you   120
O comfort my people   109
Arise, Jerusalem   110

RESPONSORIAL PSALM

Out of the depths *(Ps 129)*   43
May your love be upon us *(Ps 32)*   41
Have mercy, Lord *(Ps 50)*   46
Show us, Lord, your mercy *(Ps 84)*   38
Bring us back to you *(Ez 36)*   40
Deliver us, O God of Israel *(Ps 24)*   62
Our help is the name of the Lord *(Ps 102)*   61

SONGS DURING THE TIME ALLOWED FOR INDIVIDUAL CONFESSION

The Beatitudes   69
The Lord Jesus   82
Where there is charity and love   93
You are my servant   85
Prayer of St Francis   98
I search everywhere   91
I am the way   84
God is love   74
Christ suffered for you   120
Surely he has borne our griefs   107
Other songs may be chosen in accordance with the principles given above.

PROCLAMATION OF PRAISE

The Lourdes Magnificat   122
All you nations *(Ps 65)*   51
Alleluia *(Ps 112)*   42
Let all who are baptised   100
Christ, Our Lord, has come to save his people   81
Other songs may be chosen in accordance with the principles given above.

ANOINTING OF THE SICK

If one member of the Body of Christ suffers all the members suffer with that person. A parish can show its care and concern by gathering for a communal celebration of the anointing of the sick. This is also a recognition of the part the sick can play in the life of the parish. Songs should foster common prayer, express the Easter joy associated with the sacrament, and encourage the sick to trust in the healing power of Christ.

When the anointing of the sick takes place during the Eucharist the principles on page 9 apply. The responsorial psalm, entrance and communion songs may be chosen from the list below. Singing may also take place during the anointing.

Come, O Lord   92
Let not your hearts be troubled   86
You are my servant   85
Keep in mind   65
Come, Holy Spirit   96
Though so many, we are one   79
Christ is alive   76
Come to me   97
The Beatitudes (Refrain 1)   69
I am the bread of life   70
Gift of peace   76
Let all who are baptised   100
Christ suffered for you   120

Responsorial Psalms
My soul is longing for your peace *(Ps 131)*   55
Show us, Lord, your mercy *(Ps 84)*   38
The Lord is my shepherd *(Ps 22)*   118
Like the deer that yearns *(Ps 41-42)*   48
S'é an Tiarna m'aoire *(Ps 22)*   49
Caomhnaigh mé a Thiarna *(Ps 15)*   58
Preserve me, God *(Ps 15)*   39
Other songs may be chosen according to the principles given above.

MARRIAGE

The marriage ceremony is an occasion of joy, a celebration of the covenant of love between husband and wife. The rite emphasises the dignity of married love which is a sign of Christ's loving union with his Church.

Music has always played an important part in the celebration of marriage. However, it has tended to be regarded as merely ornamental, a pleasant "background". Some of the solo items customarily requested (e.g. "Wedding March", Mendelssohn; "Wedding March", Wagner; "Largo", Handel; "Ave Maria", Gounod; "Ave Maria", Schubert) in no way reflect the richness of the sacrament (cf. *Notitiae*, March 1971).

The principles for the use of music at the Eurcharist, page 9 ff, apply. If there is a soloist he should be encouraged to contribute to the celebration by singing the responsorial psalm and by leading the people in the acclamations. The soloist may also sing the verses of responsorial songs and encourage the people to sing the refrains. Some examples of appropriate songs are:

May Christ live in our hearts 95
God is love 74
Where there is charity 93
The Beatitudes (Refrain 1) 69
All of my life 71
How can I repay the Lord 40
I am the way (Verses 2 to 6) 84
The Lourdes Magnificat 122
Love is his word 114
This is my will 113
Hymn to love 111

Responsorial Psalms
May your love be upon us *(Ps 32)* 41
Alleluia *(Ps 112)* 42
All the earth *(Ps 99)* 54
Molaigí an Tiarna *(Ps 116)* 50
The Lord is my shepherd *(Ps 22)* 118
S'é an Tiarna m'aoire *(Ps 22)* 49
Other songs may be chosen in accordance with the principles given above.

ORDINATION TO THE PRIESTHOOD

In the sacrament of orders priests are consecrated in the image of Christ, the eternal high priest, to preach the Gospel, shepherd the faithful, and celebrate the worship of God. The gathered community prays that God will fill them with the Spirit of holiness and that they will be faithful to their ministry.

As ordination takes place within the Eucharist, the principles given on page 9 apply. Songs on the themes of "following Christ", " service", and "anointing of the Spirit" are appropriate. If there are several candidates for ordination, there may be singing, once the formula has been heard by the people, during the promise of obedience, the investiture and anointing of hands, and the kiss of peace. In order to focus attention on the solemn action being performed, it is recommended that singing not take place during the laying-on of hands. The litany of the saints (*Roman Missal*, page 208) is sung. The *Veni Creator* (*Jubilate Deo*, page 34) may be sung during the investiture and anointing of hands. The following are examples of appropriate songs:

The Lord Jesus   82
You are my servant   85
Come, Holy Spirit   96
How can I repay the Lord   40
Though so many, we are one   79
I am the way   84
Gift of peace   76
Prayer of St Francis   98
The Lourdes Magnificat   122
Dona Nobis Pacem (During the sign of peace)   83

Responsorial Psalms
The Lord is my shepherd *(Ps 22)*   118
S'é an Tiarna m'aoire *(Ps 22)*   49
All the earth *(Ps 99)*   54
Molaigí an Tiarna *(Ps 116)*   50
Jesus took bread *(Ps 33)*   42
Other appropriate songs may be chosen according to the principles given above.

RELIGIOUS PROFESSION

By religious professsion a Christian is consecrated in a special way to the service of God and the Church. His offering is united with the Eucharistic sacrifice. The gathered community commends him to God and prays that he will fulfil his dedication. The guidelines for the use of music at the celebration of the Eucharist (page 9) apply here. The following are some examples of appropriate songs:

May Christ live in our hearts   95
Without seeing you   67
How can I repay the Lord   40
God is love   74
Maranatha   63
Christ is alive   76
I am the way   84
All of my life   71
Gift of peace   76
Prayer of St Francis   98
The Lourdes Magnificat   122
The Beatitudes (Refrain 1)   69
You are my servant   85

Responsorial Psalms
May your love be upon us *(Ps 32)*   41
Like the deer that yearns *(Ps 41-42)*   48
All the earth *(Ps 99)*   54
I will celebrate *(Ps 88)*   35
Let me sing of your law *(Ps 118)*   46
Lord you have the words *(Ps 18)*   45
Behold, O Lord, I come to do your will *(Ps 39)*   60

CHRISTIAN BURIAL

The purpose of the funeral rite is to commend the dead to God, to support the Christian hope of the bereaved, and to give witness to our faith in the resurrection. Music is a powerful means of expressing Christian faith and hope. On the occasion of a funeral, however, the music should be chosen sensitively out of deference to the feelings of the mourners. A selection of the Gregorian "requiem chants", so specially suited to the funeral liturgy, will be found in *Christian Burial*. With reference to the celebration of the Eucharist, the principles on pages 9 to 23 apply. Some examples of appropriate songs are as follows:

Come to me   97
Keep in mind   65
Let not your hearts be troubled   86
The Beatitudes (Refrain 2)   69
Without seeing you   67
Priestly people   64
Maranatha   63
Dona nobis pacem   83
Gift of peace   76
How can I repay the Lord   40
I am the way   84

Responsorial Psalms
My soul is longing for your peace *(Ps 130)*   55
S'é an Tiarna m'aoire *(Ps 22)*   49
The Lord is my shepherd *(Ps 22)*   118
Preserve me, God *(Ps 15)*   39
Caomhnaigh mé a Thiarna *(Ps 15)*   58
Lord, you have the words *(Ps 18)*   45
Like the deer that yearns *(Ps 41-42)*   48
Show us, Lord, your mercy *(Ps 84)*   38
Have mercy, Lord *(Ps 50)*   46
Out of the depths *(Ps 129)*   43
Other appropriate songs may be chosen according to the principles given above.

PSALMS

I WILL CELEBRATE

Text based on
Ps 88: 2-5, 16-18, 21-22

Karen Barrie

Verses

1. I have made a co - ve - nant with my cho - sen
2. Yah - weh, the as - sem - bly of those who love you ap -
3. Hap - py the peo - ple who learn to ac - claim you, —
4. I have re - vealed my cho - sen ser - vant, and

1. gi - ven my ser - vant my word. — I have made your name to
2. plaud your mar - vel - lous word. — Who in the skies can com -
3. they re - joice in your light. — You are our glo - ry and
4. he can re - ly on me; — gi - ven him my love to

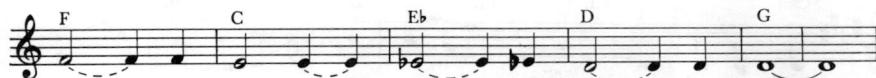

1. last for - e - ver built to out - last all time.
2. pare with Yah - weh? Who can ri - val him?
3. you are our cou - rage. Our hope be - longs to you.
4. last for e - ver He shall rise in my name.

Refrain

I will ce - le - brate your love for e - ver Yah - weh. Age on age

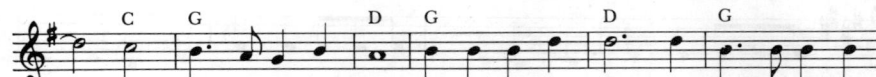

my words pro - claim your love. For I claim that love is built to last for -

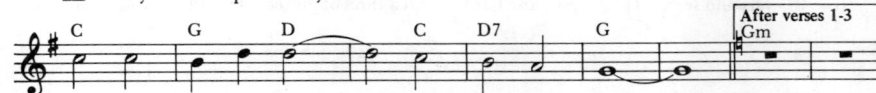

After verses 1-3

- e - ver, foun - ded firm your faith - ful - ness.

35

CANTICLE OF DANIEL

Text based on
Dan 3: 57-88, 56

Margaret Daly

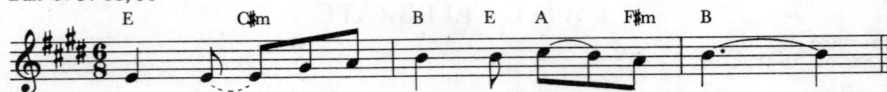

E   C#m   B   E   A   F#m   B

1. All you works of the Lord, O bless__ the Lord!_____ ℟
2. An - gels__ of the Lord, O bless __ the Lord!_____ ℟

Refrain E   F#m   E   B7   E

To him be high - est glo - ry and praise_ for e - ver.

E   C#m   F#m

3. Heav'ns of the Lord, O bless the Lord, clouds of the sky, __ O
4. Sun __ and moon, O bless the Lord, stars of the hea - vens, O
5. Bree- zes and winds, O bless the Lord, **Fire__ and heat,__** O
6. Sho- wers and dew, O bless the Lord, Frosts_ and cold, _ O
7. Night-time and day, O bless the Lord, dark-ness and light, _ O

C#m   E C#m   B E A F#m B

3. bless the Lord.__ Ar - mies_ of the Lord, O bless_ the Lord.__ ℟
4. bless the Lord, And you,__ sho-wers and rain, O bless_ the Lord.__ ℟
5. bless the Lord, And you,__ cold _ and heat, O bless_ the Lord.__ ℟
6. bless the Lord, And you,__ frost_ and snow, O bless_ the Lord.__ ℟
7. bless the Lord, And you,__ light-ning and clouds, O bless_ the Lord.__ ℟

E   A   B

8. Let__ the earth bless_ the Lord.__ ℟

9. Moun-tains and hills, O bless the Lord, Plants of the earth, O bless the Lord, and
10. Ri - vers and seas, O bless the Lord, Crea-tures of the sea, O bless the Lord,__

You _____ foun - tains and springs, O bless __ the Lord. _____ ℟
Ev' - ry bird in the sky, O bless __ the Lord. _____ ℟

11. Chil-dren of men, O bless __ the Lord. _____ ℟.

12. Is - ra - el, O bless the Lord, Priests of the Lord, O bless the Lord.

Ser - vants __ of the Lord, O bless __ the Lord. _____ ℟

13. Spi-rits and souls of the just, O bless the Lord. Ho- ly and hum-ble of heart, O

bless the Lord A - na - ni - as, A - za - ri - as, Mi- sa - el, O bless __ the Lord. __ ℟.

14. Praise the Fa - ther the Son and the Ho - ly Spi - rit. _____ ℟.

15. May you be blessed, O Lord in the hea - vens. __ ℟

37

SHOW US, LORD, YOUR MERCY

Ps 84: 8-14

Anthony Milner

Refrain

Show us, Lord, your mer - cy and grant us your sal - va - tion.

Verses

1. I will hear what the Lord has to say, a voice that speaks of peace,

peace for his peo - ple and his friends. His help is near for those who

fear him and his glo - ry will dwell in our land. ℟. 2. Mer - cy and faith-ful-ness have

met, jus - tice and peace have em - braced. Faith-ful-ness shall spring from the earth and

jus - tice look down from heaven. ℟. 3. The Lord will make us pros - per and our

earth shall yield it's fruit. Jus-tice shall march be - fore him and peace shall fol-low his steps. ℟

PRESERVE ME, GOD

Ps 15

Refrain

Pre - serve me, God, I take re - fuge in you.

Verses (These should be sung with the natural rhythm of the spoken word)

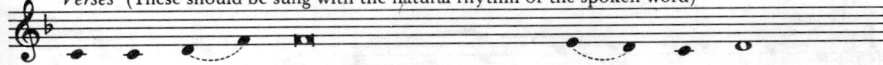

1. Pre - serve _ me, God, I take re - fuge in you.
2. He has put in - to my heart a mar - vel - lous love
3. O Lord, _ it is you who are my por - tion and cup.
4. I will bless the Lord who gives _ me counsel.
5. And so my heart rejoices, my soul _ is glad.
6. You will show _ me the path _ of life,

1. I say to the Lord, 'You are my God,
2. For the faithful ones who dwell in his land.
3. It is you your - self who are my prize.
4. Who even at night di - rects my heart.
5. E - ven my body shall rest in safety.
6. The fullness of joy in your presence.

1. My happiness lies in you _ a - lone'. ℟
2. Those who choose other gods in - crease _ their sorrows.
3. The lot marked out for me is my _ de - light.
4. I keep the Lord ever in _ my sight.
5. For you will not leave my soul a - mong _ the dead.
6. At your right hand, happi - ness _ for ever. ℟

2. Ne - ver will _ I of - fer their of - fer - ings of blood.

2. Ne - ver will _ I take their name on my lips. ℟
3. Wel - come in - deed _ the heritage that falls _ to me. ℟
4. Since he is at my right hand, I shall stand firm. ℟
5. Nor let your be - lo - ved know _ de - cay. ℟

39

BRING US BACK TO YOU, O LORD OUR GOD

Ez 35: 24-28

Paul Décha

Refrain

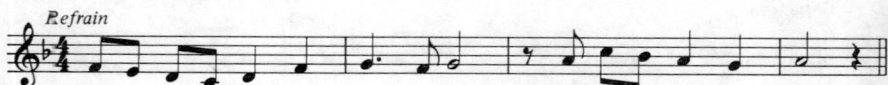

Bring us back to you, O Lord our God, and save us in your name.

Verses

1. I will ga - ther you from the na - tions, and I will u -
2. I will pour on you li - ving wa - ter. I will make you
3. I will take the heart you have har - dened. I will put in
4. In your soul my Spi - rit will dwell ___ and he will re -
5. I will be your Fa - ther for e - ver. You will al - ways

1. nite you in my love. ___ This is the word of God. ℟
2. clean and pure of heart. ___ This is the word of God. ℟
3. you a heart of flesh. ___ This is the word of God. ℟
4. veal my will to you. ___ This is the word of God. ℟
5. be my cho - sen peo - ple. This is the word of God. ℟

HOW CAN I REPAY THE LORD

Ps 115: 12-19

Colin Mawby

1. How can I re - pay the Lord for his good - ness to me?
2. My vows to the Lord I will ful - fil before all his peo - ple.
3. Your servant, Lord, your ser - vant am I; you have loo - sened my bonds.
4. My vows to the Lord I will ful - fil before all his peo - ple,

1. The cup of sal - va - tion _ I will raise; I will call _ on the Lord's name.
2. O precious in __ the __ eyes of the Lord is the death of his faith - ful.
3. A thanksgiving sa - cri - fice I make; I will call on the Lord's name.
4. In the courts of the house of the Lord, In your midst, O Je - ru - sa - lem.

40

MAY YOUR LOVE BE UPON US

Ps 32: 4-5, 18-22

Margaret Daly

Refrain

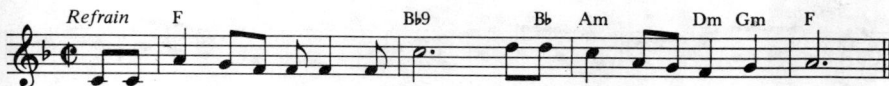

May your love be u - pon us, O Lord, as we place all our hope in you.

Verses

1. For the word of the Lord __ is __ faith - ful, and
2. The __ Lord looks on those __ who re - vere him, on
3. Our __ soul __ is wai - ting for the Lord; __ the

1. all __ his works to be trus - ted. The Lord loves __ jus - tice and
2. those __ who hope in his love, __ to res - cue their souls __ from
3. Lord is our help and our shield, __ in him do our hearts __ find

1. right and fills __ the earth with his love. __ ℟
2. death, to keep them a - live __ in fa - mine. ℟
3. joy; we trust in his ho - ly name. __ ℟

Other appropriate psalm verses may be sung to the following melody with
the refrain 'May your love be upon us'.

Laurence Bevenot O.S.B.

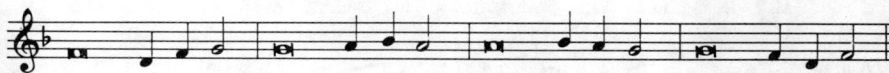

41

JESUS TOOK BREAD

Mk 14: 22. Ps 33: 9-10, 17-19
Adapted by Harold Winstone

Kevin Mayhew

Refrain

Je - sus took bread and blessed and broke it and said, 'Take, eat, this is my bo - dy'.

Verses

C   Am   G

1.   Taste   and   see   how   good   he   is;   how
2. Fear   the   Lord,   you   his   ho -   ly   ones
3. When the   just   cry   out   the   Lord   hears
4.   Their hearts may be   bro - ken, but   he   is   close   by;   their

Dm   G7   C

1. hap - py   the   man   who   puts   his   trust   in   the   Lord.   ℞
2.   for   those   who   fear him   will   want   for   no - thing. ℞
3.   he   res - cues   them   from   all their   dis - tress.   ℞
4. spi -rits may be crushed   but   he   will   save   them   all.   ℞

ALLELUIA

Text composite
based on Ps 112

Paul Décha

Refrain

Al - le - lu - ia,   Al - le - lu - ia,   Al - le - lu - ia.

Verses

1. O   ser-vants of   God give him praise; Give him praise ac- know-ledge his   name. ___ ℞
2. O blest be the name of the   Lord, May cre - a - tion re-sound with his   praise. ___ ℞
3. The Lord reigns in   glo - ry   on high, From his throne he sees hea- ven and   earth. ___ ℞
4. He rai - ses the   poor from the   dust, And like prin - ces they dwell in the   land. ___ ℞
5. Our sons are a   gift from the Lord. He gives chil-dren to   glad-den our   hearts. ___ ℞
6. Come tell of the great-ness of   God, And re -joice as you ring out his   praise. ___ ℞

Other appropriate psalm verses may be sung to the
following melody with the refrain 'Alleluia'.

Fintan O'Carroll

OUT OF THE DEPTHS

Ps 129

Joseph Gelineau

Refrain

I place all my trust in you, my God: all my hope is in your sa - ving word.

Verses

1. Out of the **depths**   I **cry** to you,   O **Lord,**
2. If you, O **Lord,**   should **mark**   our **guilt,**
3. My **soul**   is **waiting** for the **Lord,**   I
4. Be - **cause**   with the **Lord** there is **mercy,**   and

1. **Lord** hear my **voice.**   O **let** your **ears** be at -
2. **Lord,** who would sur - **vive?**   But with **you** is **found** for -
3. **count** on his **word:**   My **soul** is **longing** for the
4. **fullness** of re - **demption.**   **Israel** in - **deed** he will re-

1. -**ten**tive   to the **voice** of my **plead** - ing. ℟
2. -**giveness**   for **this** we re - **vere** you. ℟
3. **Lord**   more than **watch** - man for **day** - break. ℟
4. -**deem**   from **all** its in - **iq** - uity. ℟

Other appropriate psalm verses may be sung to the following
melody with the refrain - 'I place all my trust in you, my God'.

Laurence Bevenot O.S.B.

43

SING A NEW SONG TO THE LORD

Text based on Ps 97
Timothy Dudley-Smith

David G. Wilson

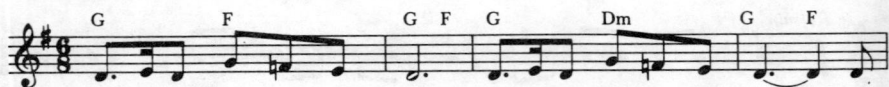

1. Sing a new song to the Lord, He to whom won-ders be - long! __ Re-
2. Now to the ends of the earth, See his sal - va - tion is shown:__ And
3. Sing a new song and re - joice. Pub-lish his prai-ses a - broad!__ Let
4. Join with the hills and the sea. Thun-ders of praise to pro - long. __ In

1. joice_____ in his tri - umph__ and tell_____ of his power. __ O
2. still_____ he re - mem-bers__ his mer - cy and truth,__ Un-
3. voi - ces____ in__ cho - rus__ with trum- pet__ and __ horn.__ Re-
4. judge - ment __ and jus - tice____ He comes_____ to the earth, __ O

Verses 1-3   Verse 4

1. sing_____ to the Lord_____ a new song.
2. -chan - ging in love_____ to his own.
3. sound____ for the joy____ of the Lord.
4. sing_____ to the Lord_____ a new song.

SING TO THE LORD

John Foley SJ
based on Ps 95
Refrain

John Foley SJ

Sing to the Lord, Al - le - lu - ia, sing to the Lord.

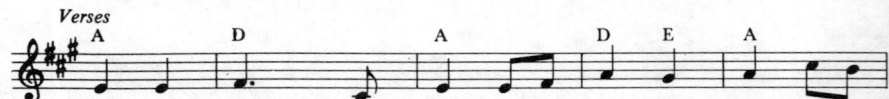

Verses

1. Bless his name, an - nounce his sal - va - tion day af - ter
2. Give to him, you fam' - lies of peo - ples glo - ry and
3. Great is he, and wor - thy of prai - ses day af - ter
4. He it is who gave us the hea - vens; glo - ry to
5. Tell his glo - ries, tell all the na - tions, day af - ter
6. Bring your gifts and en - ter his tem - ple wor - ship the

44

F#m　　　B　　　　E　　　　A

1. day,　　al - le - lu - ia. _____ ℟.
2. praise,　al - le - lu - ia. _____ ℟.
3. day,　　al - le - lu - ia. _____ ℟.
4. God,　　al - le - lu - ia. _____ ℟.
5. day,　　al - le - lu - ia. _____ ℟.
6. Lord,　al - le - lu - ia. _____ ℟.

LORD, YOU HAVE THE WORDS OF EVERLASTING LIFE

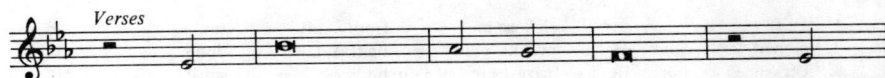

Jn 6: 68, Ps 18: 8-11

C. Alexander Peloquin

Refrain

Lord, you have the words of e - ver - last - ing life.

Verses

1. The law of the Lord is perfect, it re -
2. The precepts of the Lord are right, they
3. The fear of the Lord is holy, a -
4. They are more to be de -sired than gold, than the

1. -vives the soul. The rule of the Lord is to be
2. glad-den the heart. The com - mand of the Lord _ is ___
3. - bi - ding for - ever. The de - crees of the Lord _ are ___
4. pur - est ___ of gold, and sweeter are they _ than __

1. trusted, it gives wisdom to the simple. ℟
2. clear, it gives. light to the eyes. ℟
3. truth, and __ all of them __ just. ℟
4. honey, than __ honey from the comb. ℟

45

HAVE MERCY LORD

Ps 50: 3-6, 12-13, 16-17

Joseph Gelineau

Refrain

Have mer - cy Lord, cleanse me from all __ my sins.

Verses

1. Have mercy on me God in your kindness In your com - passion blot
2. My of - fences truly I know them; my sin is
3. A pure heart cre - ate for me, O God, put a steadfast
4. Give me a - gain the joy of your help; with a spirit of

1. out of my of - fence O wash me more and more from my
2. always be - fore me Against you, you a - lone have I
3. spirit with - in me. Do not cast me a - way from your
4. fervour sus - tain me. O Lord, open my

1. guilt and cleanse me from my sin. ℟
2. sinned what is evil in your sight I have done. ℟
3. presence nor de - prive me of your ho-ly spirit. ℟
4. lips and my mouth shall de - clare your praise. ℟

LET ME SING OF YOUR LAW

Text adapted from
Ps 118: 25-32

Lucien Deiss

Refrain

E7 A D E A D

Let me sing of your law, O my God ____ Let your

Bm C#m F#m E *Verses* A

love __ come u - pon your peo - ple.

1. Through your own
2. Show me the
3. O take me
4. With - in your
5. My heart is

46

1. word,	Lord, give us life.	In your ho - ly kee - ping	hap - py is my soul. ℟
2. way	to keep your law.	Let your ho - ly pre - cepts	dwell with-in my mind. ℟
3. far	from e - vil ways.	And in your great mer - cy	guide me in your paths. ℟
4. law	I choose to live.	In the paths of wis - dom	I walk e - ver-more. ℟
5. strong,	my joy is full.	Fol-low - ing your law, Lord	free - ly do I walk. ℟

JESUS CHRIST IS LORD

Text based on
Phil 2: 11, Ps 144: 1-11

Mary Mc Cooey

Refrain

Je - sus Christ is lord. He is lord to the

glo - ry of God the Fa - ther.

Verses

1.	Glo -	ry	to	you,	O	God our	King
2.	Blest	be	the	lord		day	af - ter day.
3. The	lord	is		great,		high - ly to be	praised.
4.	Age	to		age	pro -	claims your	works,
5. Let	all	men		tell	the	deeds of the	lord,
6. The	lord	is		kind,	a -	bound - ing in	love,

1. Blest	be your	name	for	e -	ver.	℟
2. Praise	his sur - pas -	sing	great -	ness.		℟
3. No	one could mea - sure	his	splen -	dour.		℟
4. All	of the	earth	your	glo -	ry.	℟
5. All	men shall praise	his	glo -	ry.		℟
6. Je -	sus is	our	re -	dee -	mer.	℟

LIKE THE DEER THAT YEARNS

Ps 41:1, 42:3—4

Joseph Walshe

Refrain

Like the deer that yearns for run - ning streams

so my soul is year - ning for you, my God.

Verses

1. My soul is thirst - ing for God, the God of my life
When can I enter and see the face of God? R.

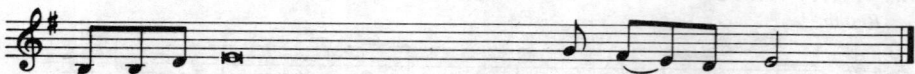

2. O send forth your light and your truth, let these be my guide
Let them bring me to your ho - ly moun - tain, to the place where you dwell. R.

3. And I will come to the al - tar of God, the God of my joy,
my re dee - mer I will thank you on the harp, O God my God. R.

'SÉ AN TIARNA M'AOIRE

Salm 22

Fiontán P. O Cearbhaill

Freagra

'Sé an Tiar - na m'aoi - re; ní bheidh aon ní de dhíth orm.

Cantóir

1. 'Sé an Tiar - na m'aoi - re; ní bheidh aon ní de
2. Seo-lann sé me ar rian - ta dí - rea - cha mar gheall ar a
3.
4.

1. dhíth orm. Cui-reann sé 'mo luí me i
2. ainm. Fiú da siúl - - fainn i ngleann an dor - cha - dais, níor
3. Cói - ríonn tú bord chun béi - le dom i
4. Lean-faidh cin - eál - - tas is fá - bhar me gach

1. móin - éar féar - ghlas; seo-lann sé ar i - meall an
2. bhaol liom an t-olc; a - gus tú fa - ram le do
3. bhfian - ai - se mo naimh - de; un-gann tú mo cheann le
4. uile lá de mo shaol; i dteach an Tiar - na a

1. uis - ce me, mar a bhfaigh - - im suaimh - neas. F
2. shlat is do bha-chall, chun só - lás a thabhairt dom. F
3. ho - la; tá mo chu-pán ag cur thar mhaoil F
4. mhair - fidh me go brách na breithe. F

Other appropriate psalm verses may be sung to the following
melody with the refrain 'Se an Tiarna M'aoire'.

Stanbrook 7E

YES, I SHALL ARISE

Lk 15: 18
Verses from the penitential psalms

Lucien Deiss

Refrain

E   B   C#m   G#m   E   Amaj7   E

Yes I shall a - rise, and re - turn to my Fa - ther.

Verses

E   G#m   A   F#m

1.	To	you,	O	Lord,	I	lift	up	my	soul.	In	you,	O	my
2.	Look	down	on	me,	have	mer -	cy,	O	Lord.	For -	give	me	my
3.	Do	not	with -	hold	your	good -	ness from		me.	O	Lord,	may	your
4.	Mer -	cy,	I	cry,	O	Lord,	wash me		clean.	And	whi -	ter	than
5.	Give	me	a -	gain	the	joy	of	your	help.	Now	o -	pen	my
6.	My	soul	will	sing,	my	heart	will	re -	joice.	The	bles -	sings	of

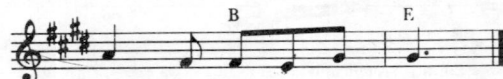

B   E

1.	God,	I	place	all	my	trust.	℟
2.	sins,	be -	hold	all	my	grief.	℟
3.	love	be	deep	in	my	soul.	℟
4.	snow	my	spi -	rit	shall	be.	℟
5.	lips,	your	praise	I	will	sing.	℟
6.	God	will	fill	all	my	days.	℟

MOLAIGÍ AN TIARNA, ALLELUIA

Salm 116

Kevin Healey O.S.B.

Freagra

Mol - ai - gí an Tiar - na, al - le - lu - ia.

Cantóir

3

(Pobal)

Molaigí an Tiarna, an chin - ío - cha go léir Al - le - lu - ia.

Cantóir

Molaigí É, a ná-siúin ui - le. F.

50

Óir bíonn carthanacht trocaireach dúinn ag dul i méid i gcó - naí, Al - le - lu - ia.

Cantóir

Agus maireann fírinne an Tiar - na go deo. F.

Other appropriate psalm verses may be sung to the following
melody with the refrain 'Molaigí an Tiarna'.

Fintan O'Carroll

ALL YOU NATIONS

Ps. 65

Lucien Deiss

Refrain

All you na-tions sing out your joy to the Lord, al - le - lu - ia, al - le - lu - ia.

Verses

1. Joy - ful - ly shout. All you on earth, give praise to the glo - ry of God;
2. Let all the earth kneel in his sight ex - tol - ling his mar - vel - lous fame;
3. Come forth and see all the great works that God has brought forth by his might;
4. Par - ting the seas with might and power, he res - cued his peo - ple from shame;
5. Glo - ry and thanks be to the Fa - ther; ho-nour and praise to the Son;

1. And with a hymn, sing out _ his glo- ri - ous praise: Al - le - lu - ia. ℟
2. Ho-nour his name, in high - est hea-ven give praise; Al - le - lu - ia. ℟
3. Fall on your knees be - fore _ his glo- ri-ous throne; Al - le - lu - ia. ℟
4. Let us give thanks for all _ his mer- ci - ful deeds; Al - le - lu - ia. ℟
5. And to the Spi - rit, source of life and of love; Al - le - lu - ia. ℟

Other appropriate psalm verses may be sung to the following
melody with the refrain 'All you nations'.

Anon

GIVE PRAISE TO THE LORD ALL YOU MEN

Ps 112

Lucien Deiss

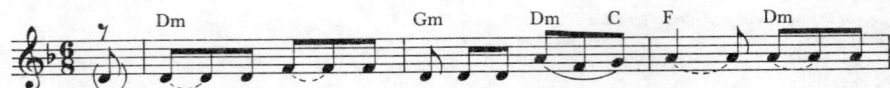

1. Give praise to the Lord all you men, al - le - lu - ia, O praise the
2. Now and e - ver more al - le - lu - ia; From dawn to

1. name of the Lord, al - le - lu - ia. Blessed be the name of the
2. close of the day, al - le - lu - ia. Blessed be the name of the

1. Lord, al - le - lu - ia. Al - le - lu - ia!
2. Lord, al - le - lu - ia. Al - le - lu - ia!

3. On high a - bove the earth is the Lord, al - le - lu - ia! His glo - ry a -

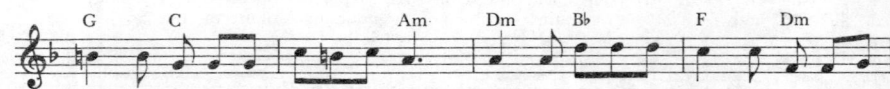

- bove the sky, al - le - lu - ia. There is none like the Lord our God, al - le -

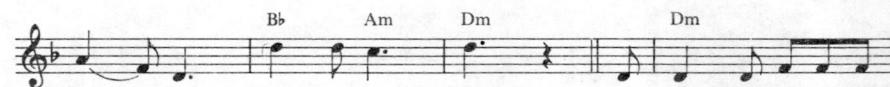

lu - ia. Al - le - lu - ia! 4 En - throned in hea - ven on

52

Gm   Dm   C   F   Dm   G   C   Am

high, al - le - lu - ia, he views the earth and the sky, al - le - lu - ia to

Dm   Bb   F   Dm   Bb   Am   Dm

those in need he gives his help, al - le - lu - ia, al - le - lu - ia.

Dm   C   Dm   Gm   Dm   C F   Dm   G

5. From the dust he rai - ses the poor al - le - lu - ia, He makes them sit a-mong

C   Am   Bb   F   Dm

kings al - le - lu - ia; a-mong the kings of the earth, al - le - lu - ia,

Bb   Am   Dm   Dm   Gm   Dm   C

al - le - lu - ia.   6. Be - hold the bar - ren wife, al - le - lu -
7. Let us sing to the Lord, al - le - lu -

F   Dm   G   C   Am   Dm   Bb

6. ia. Now a - bides in her home, al - le - lu - ia, ____ As the hap - py
7. ia. Sing - ing glo - ry and praise al - le - lu - ia, Both now and e - ver

F   Dm   Bb   Am   Dm

6. mo-ther of sons, al - le - lu - ia, Al - le - lu - ia. ____
7. more, ___ A - men, al - le - lu - ia, Al - le - lu - ia. ____

ALL THE EARTH PROCLAIM THE LORD

Ps 99

Lucien Deiss

Refrain

All the earth pro - claim_ the Lord, sing your praise to God.

Verses

1. Serve you the Lord, heart filled with glad - ness, Come
2. Know that the Lord is our cre - a - tor. Yes
3. We are the sheep of his green pas - ture, For
4. En - ter his gates bring - ing thanks - gi - ving, O
5. Our Lord is good, his love en - du - ring, His
6. Ho - nour and praise be to the Fa - ther, The

1. in - to his pre - sence sing - ing for joy! ℞
2. he is our Fa - ther, we are his sons. ℞
3. we are his peo - ple, he is our God. ℞
4. en - ter his courts while sing - ing his praise. ℞
5. word is a - bi - ding now with all men. ℞
6. Son and the Spi - rit, world with - out end. ℞

PSALM 150

Text adapted by
Omer Westendorf

Jan Vermulst

Refrain

Al - le - lu - ia, Al - le - lu - ia, Al - le - lu - ia.

Verses

1. Praise God __ in his Ho - ly dwel - ling; Praise him __ on his
2. Praise him __ with the blast _ of trum - pet; Praise him __ now with
3. Praise him __ with re - soun - ding cym - bals; With cym - bals that
4. Praise God __ the al - migh - ty Fa - ther; Praise Christ __ his be -

54

1. migh - ty throne; Praise him ___ for his won - der - ful deeds;
2. lyre ___ and harps; Praise him ___ with the tim - brel and dance;
3. crash ___ give praise; O let ___ ev' - ry - thing that has breath,
4. -lo - ved Son; Give Praise ___ to the Spi - rit of love.

1. Praise him ___ for his sov' - reign ma - jes - ty. ℟
2. Praise him ___ with the sound of string ___ and reed. ℟
3. Let all ___ li - ving crea - tures Praise ___ the Lord. ℟
4. For e - ver the tri - une God ___ be praised ℟

MY SOUL IS LONGING FOR YOUR PEACE

Ps 131   Lucien Deiss

My soul is long - ing for your peace, near to you my God.

1. Lord, you know that my heart is not proud, and my eyes are
2. Lof - ty thoughts have ne - ver filled my mind, far be - yond my
3. In your peace I have main - tained my soul I have kept my
4. As a child rests on his mo - thers knee, So I place my
5. Is - ra - el, put all your hope in God. Place your trust in

1. not lif - ted from the earth. ℟
2. sight all am - bi - tious deeds. ℟
3. heart in your qui - et peace. ℟
4. soul in your lo - ving care. ℟
5. him, now and e - ver - more. ℟

Other appropriate psalm verses may be sung to the following   Gabriel I
melody with the refrain 'My soul is longing for your peace'.

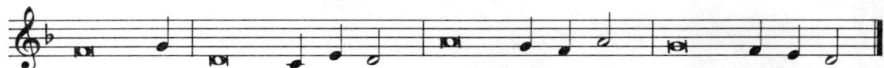

GRANT TO US, O LORD

Ez 36: 26, Jer 31: 31-34 Lucien Deiss

Refrain

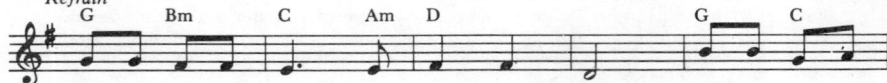

Grant to us, O Lord a heart re - newed; re - cre -ate in

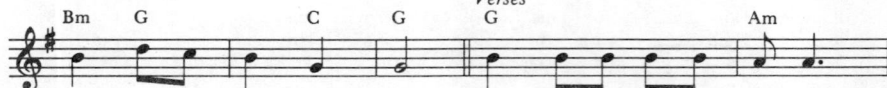

us your own Spi - rit, Lord! 1. Be - hold the days are co - ming

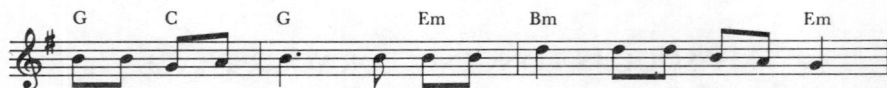

says the Lord our God when I will make a new co - ve - nant

with the house of___ Is - ra - el. ℟ 2. Deep with-in their be - ing I will im -

- plant my___ law; I will write it on their hearts. ℟ 3. I will be their

God, and they shall be my___ peo - ple. ℟ 4. And for all their faults I will

grant for - give - ness; ne - ver - more will I re - mem - ber their sins. ℟

I WANT TO SING

Ps 56: 8-10

Lucien Deiss

Refrain

I want to sing, I want to shout your praise, ___ O Lord!

A - wake_ and sing my soul.___ A - wake_ and

play my harp_ and _ zi - ther! Let the dawning day join _ in ___ praise.

Verses

1. My heart is rea - dy now to praise_ you, O Lord,
2. For great and won - der - ful your glo - ry, my God;
3. Lord, your mer - cy o - ver - sha - dows the earth;

1. to bless you God of my sal - va - tion, Al-le - lu - ia. ℟
2. your name is great a - bove the hea - vens, Al-le - lu - ia. ℟
3. your glo - ry lights the fir - mament on high, Al-le - lu - ia. ℟

57

CAOMHNAIGH MÉ A THIARNA

Salm 15

Séan Óg Ó Tuama

Freagra

Caomh-naigh mé a Thiar - na is ort - sa a thriall - aim.

Bhéarsaí

1. Is é an Tiarna is rogha liom; mo chuid de réir oidhreachta,
2. Tá gairdeas ar mo chroí agus áth - as ar m'anam,
3. Taispéanfaidh tú slí na beath - a dom,

1. agus cuid mo chailíse: is ort a - tá mo sheasamh!
2. agus mairfidh mo cholainn faoi shuaimh - neas freisin.
3. agus iomlán lúch - áire i d'fhian - aise,

1. Coiméadaim an Tiar - na de shíor os mo choinne
2. Óir ní fhágfaidh tú m'an - am i measc na marbh:

1. agus é ar mo dheasláimh ní chorr - - ó - far mé choíche. F.
2. ná ní ligfidh tú do do mhuirneach truaill - iú a fheiceáil. F.
3. agus aoibhneas ar do dheas - láimh go brách. F.

Other appropriate psalm verses may be sung to the following
melody with the refrain 'Caomhnaigh mé a Thiarna'.

Fintan O'Carroll

58

ALLELUIA

Ps 148

David Julien

Refrain

Al - le - lu - ia Al - le - lu - ia, Al - le - lu - ia.

Verses

1.	Praise	the Lord	from the	heav'ns	praise	him	in the	heights	Al - le - lu -
2.	Praise	the Lord,	sun and	moon	praise	him shin-ing	stars,		Al - le - lu -
3.	Let	them praise	his	name,	he spoke	and they were made,			Al - le - lu -
4.	Let	the earth	praise the	Lord,	all crea - tures	of the	sea,		Al - le - lu -
5.	All	the moun - tains and	hills,	all fruit		trees and cedars,			Al - le - lu -
6.	All	earth's peo - ples and	kings,	the prin -	ces	and rulers,			Al - le - lu -
7.	May	the Lord's name	be	praised, his name		and no	other,		Al - le - lu -
8.	He	is strength to	his	saints, the praise	of	all his	peo - ple,	Al - le - lu -

- ia.	1.	O	Praise him	all his	an -	gels,	praise him all his
- ia.	2.	O	praise him	high-est	heav'ns, and		wa - ters in the
- ia.	3.	He	fixed	them for	e - ver,	by	his e - ter - nal
- ia.	4. fire and	hail,		snow and mist,	the		winds that do his
- ia.	5.	all	beasts	wild and tame,	all		birds on the
- ia.	6.	the	young men	and the	mai - dens, the		old men and
- ia.	7.	for	greater	is his	name	than	hea - ven and
- ia.	8.	He is	close	to his	peo - ple, the		sons of Is - ra -

1.	host,
2.	heav'ns
3.	law
4.	will
5.	wing
6.	chil dren
7.	earth
8.	el.

Al - le - lu - ia, Al - le - lu - ia. ℞.

59

BEHOLD, O LORD, I COME TO DO YOUR WILL

Ps 39:2, 4, 7—11, 17

Margaret Daly

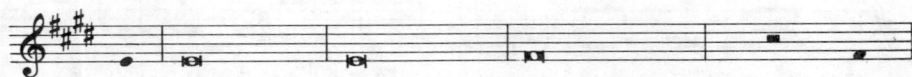

Refrain

Be - hold, O Lord, I come to do your will

1. I waited. I waited for the Lord and he
2. You do not ask for sacrifice and offerings, but an
3. In the scroll of the book it stands written that I should
4. Your justice I have pro – claimed in the
5. I have not hid - den your justice in my heart, but de -
6. O let there be re - joicing and gladness, for

1. stooped down to me; He put a new song in my
2. o – pen ear. You do not ask for holocaust and
3. do your will. My God, I de - light in your
4. great as - sembly. My lips I have not
5. clared your faith - ful help. I have not hidden your love and your
6. all who seek you. Let them say, "The Lord is

rall.

1. mouth, praise of our God. ℟.
2. victim. In - stead, here am I. ℟.
3. law. In the depth of my heart. ℟.
4. sealed; you know it, O Lord. ℟.
5. truth from the great as - sembly. ℟.
6. great," who love your sa - ving help. ℟.

60

OUR HELP IS THE NAME OF THE LORD

Oosterhuis/McGoldrick
based on Ps 102

Bernard Huijbers

Antiphon

Our — help is the name of the Lord, ——— who made — the
earth and the hea - vens —— T'ward us he is a most
mer - ci - ful fa - ther and his fi - de - li - ty knows no end.

Refrain

OUR HELP IS THE NAME OF THE LORD, AND HIS FI — DE - LI-TY KNOWS NO END.

Verses

1. He calls to me: 'Come forth from your grave'. He fills my days with
good -ness and love and like an ea - gle, my youth re - turns. ℟.

2. He does not haunt us with our — sins; He will not re-pay
e - vil with e - vil for he is grea - ter than our— sins. ℟.

3. Just as a man is mer - ci - ful to his— sons, so is he a
mer - ci - ful Fa-ther to us be -cause he made us and knows us— well.

All repeat *Antiphon* and then *Refrain*

61

DELIVER US, O GOD OF ISRAEL

Text based on Ps 24

John Foley SJ

Verses

1. Re - mem - ber that your com - pas - sion, O
2. Let us walk, Lord, a - long the path - way of your
4. Give glo - ry un - to the Fa - ther and the

1. Lord, and your kind - ness are from of old, let
2. joy. Let us find the truth from of old. For you
4. son, and the spi - rit dwel - ling with - in through

1. not our en - e - mies ex - ult o - ver us
2. guide the hum - ble in the ways of your love
4. all the ag - es to the end of all time

Refrain

De - liv - er us, O God of Is - ra - el, from all our trib - u - la - tions; de - liv - er us, O God of Is - ra - el.

Verse 3

3. To you, we lift our soul, O Lord: in you, O God we trust, let us not be put to shame. R.

62

HYMNS AND BIBLICAL SONGS

MARANATHA

2 Cor 16: 22
Ap 22: 16-17, 20

Lucien Deiss

Refrain

| E | F#m | C#m | A | G#m | C#m | B7 | E |

Ma - ra - na - tha! Come, O Christ the Lord.

Verses

| C#m | E | A | C#m | Emaj7 | B | A | E |

1. I am the root of Jes - se and Da - vid's Son, the ra - diant star of

| B | B | F#m | G#m | C#m | G#m | C#m | F#m | E |

mor-ning and God's own light. ℟ 2.The Spi- rit and the Bride say, 'Come'. Let

| A | E | F#m | C#m | G#m | C#m | G#m |

him who hears their voi - ces say, 'Come'. ℟ 3. He who has thirst let him

| G#m | A | E | B | F | C#m |

come, and he who has de - sire, let him drink the wa - ters of

| B | C#m7 | G# m | C#m | E | F#m | C#m |

e - ver - las - ting life. ℟ 4. 'Yes, I come ve - ry soon,' A -

| B | G#m | E | A | G#m | E | C#m | B | C#m |

- - - men. Come, O Lord Je - sus. ℟

63

PRIESTLY PEOPLE

Lucien Deiss

Refrain

Priest - ly peo - ple, King - ly peo - ple, Ho - ly peo - ple,

God's cho - sen peo - ple, sing praise to the Lord.

Verses

1. We sing to you, O Christ be - lov - ed Son of the Fa - ther.
2. We sing to you, O Son born of Ma - ry the Vir - gin.
3. We sing to you, O bright - ness of splen - dour and glo - ry.
4. We sing to you, O light bring - ing men out of dark - ness.
5. We sing to you, Mes - si - ah fore - told by the pro - phets.

1. We give you praise, O Wis - dom e - ver - last - ing and Word of God. ℟
2. We give you praise, our bro - ther born to heal us, our sa - ving Lord. ℟
3. We give you praise, O mor - ning star an - nounc - ing the co - ming day. ℟
4. We give you praise, O gui - ding light who shows us the way to heav'n. ℟
5. We give you praise, O Son of Da - vid and Son of Ab - ra - ham. ℟

6. We sing to you, Mes-si-ah, the hope of the people,
   We give you praise, O Christ, our Lord and King, hum-ble, meek of heart.

7. We sing to you, The Way to the Fa-ther in heav-en.
   We give you praise. The Way of Truth, and Way of all grace and light.

8. We sing to you, O Priest of the new dis-pen-sa-tion,
   We give you praise, Our Peace, sealed by the blood of the Sac-ri-fice.

9. We sing to you, O Lamb, put to death for sin-ner.
   We sing you praise, O Vic-tim, im-mo-lat-ed for all man-kind.

10. We sing to you, The Tab-er-nac-le made by the Father.
    We give you praise, The Cor-ner-stone and Sav-iour of Is-ra-el.

11. We sing to you, The Shep-herd who leads to the king-dom.
    We give you praise, Who gath-er all your sheep in the one true fold.

12. We sing to you, O Fount, o-ver-flowing with mer-cy.
    We give you praise. Who give us liv-ing wa-ters to quench our thirst.

13. We sing to you, True Vine, plant-ed by God our Father.
    We give you praise, O bless-ed Vine, whose branch-es bear fruit in love.

14. We sing to you, O Man-na, which God gives his peo-ple
    We give you praise, O liv-ing Bread, which comes down to us from heaven.

15. We sing to you, The Im-age of Fa-ther e-ter-nal.
    We give you praise, O King of justice, Lord, and the King of peace.

16. We sing to you, The First-born of all God's cre-a-tion.
    We give you praise, Sal-va-tion of your saints sleep-ing in the Lord.

17. We sing to you, O Lord, whom the Fa-ther ex-alt-ed.
    We give you praise, in glory you are com-ing to judge all men.

KEEP IN MIND

2 Tim 2: 8-11   Lucien Deiss

Refrain

Keep in mind that Je - sus Christ has died for us and is ri - sen from the
dead. He is our sa - ving Lord; he is joy for all a - ges.

Verses

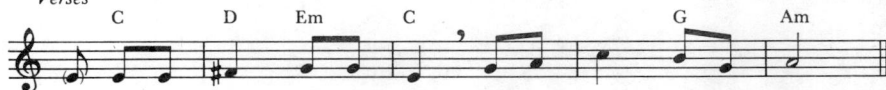

1.   If   we   die   with the   Lord,   we shall   live   with the   Lord. (℞)
2. If   we   en - dure with the   Lord,   we shall   reign with the   Lord. ℞

3. In   him   all   our   sor - row,   in   him   all   our   joy.   (℞)
4. In   him   hope of   glo - ry,   in   him   all   our   love. ℞
5. In   him   our   re - demp - tion, in   him   all   our   grace. (℞)
6. In   him   our   sal - va - tion,   in   him   all   our   peace. ℞

65

HEAVENS, DROP DEW FROM ABOVE

Is 45: 8, 'O' Antiphons

Lucien Deiss

Refrain

A	D	A	F#m	B m	C#m	F#m	D	A	Bm	C#m

Hea-vens drop dew from a - bove. Let the earth o - pen up, And the Saviour spring forth.

Verses

A	F#m		Bm	A	C#m

1.   O —— Lord,   O   Shepherd of   Israel's   house, you who
2.   O —— Wisdom that came   forth from the   mouth of the most high,   Fore -
3.   O Da-vid's Son,   the   shield of   peoples   and Kings,   The
4.   O Ri-sing Sun,   O   splendour of ever - lasting   light,   And
5.   O   Em-man-u - el   our   King,   and   Hope of the   nations, And re

F#m	Bm	Bm7	A	A			

1.   guide your ho - ly   peo - ple,   O come, re-deem us   all   By your   migh-ty
2.   told by ma - ny   pro - phets,   O come and show us   all   The way that   leads us
3. whole world calls u - pon you;   O come, de - li - ver   us,   Delay not your   co-ming,
4.   bril-liant Sun of   jus - tice;   O come and shed your light Upon those who live in the night of
5. - dee-mer of all   peo - ples;   O come to save us   all,   Delay not your   co-ming,

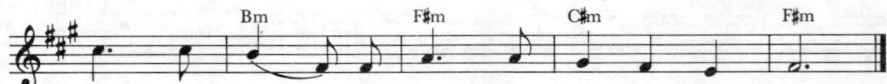

Bm	F#m	C#m	F#m

1.   arm;   O   come, —— O   Lord,   to   save   us,   O   come.   ℞
2.   home;   O   come, —— O   Lord,   to   save   us,   O   come.   ℞
3.   Lord;   O   come, —— O   Lord,   to   save   us,   O   come.   ℞
4.   death;   O   come, —— O   Lord,   to   save   us,   O   come.   ℞
5.   Lord;   O   come, —— O   Lord,   to   save   us,   O   come.   ℞

WITHOUT SEEING YOU

Refrain adapted from 1 Pet: 1-8

Lucien Deiss

Refrain

With-out see - ing you we love you; with - out see - ing you we be - lieve.

And we sing, Lord in joy your glo - ry. You are our Sa - viour we ___

___ be - lieve ___ in you.

Verses

1. Blessed is he who will lis - ten to your
2. He who lives in the Spi - rit of the
3. By our faith you a - bide with - in our
4. All my faith is in him who died for
5. By your grace you have saved us from our
6. In our hearts may the fire of love still
7. May we live in the brightness of your
8. Re - u - nite all your peo - ple in one

1. Word; ___ he shall tru - ly ne - ver see death, for by
2. Word ___ he shall find his true life in you, and the
3. hearts ___ keep us safe - ly with you in love. Give to
4. me ___ for it is not I now who live. It is
5. sins ___ in our hearts you nou - rish our faith. Our sal -
6. burn. ___ Here you give your Spi - rit to men and the
7. joy; ___ May we know the peace of your love, May we
8. faith. ___ Lead us all to hea - ven - ly joy. We will

1. you, he is heir to a new ___ life. O Lord, ___ to whom
2. truth of your word makes him free, Lord.
3. men all the hope of your power, Lord.
4. Christ now in me, my sal - va - tion.
5. - va - tion is wrought by your mer - cy.
6. flame of that fire fills the whole world.
7. sing of your glo - ry for - e - ver.
8. see your ___ face for all a - ges.

shall we go ___ You a - lone have the words of e - ter - nal life. ℟.

67

YOU ARE THE HONOUR

Jdt 15: 9-10

Lucien Deiss

Refrain

You are the ho - nour, you are the glo - ry of our peo - ple

Ho - ly Vir - gin Ma - ry.

Verses

Refrain

1. You are the glo - ry of Je - ru - sa - lem   Ho - ly Vir - gin Ma - ry.
2. You are the grea-test joy of Is - ra - el,   Ho - ly Vir - gin Ma - ry.
3. You are the high-est ho - nour of our race   Ho - ly Vir - gin Ma - ry.

Repeat - 'You are the honour' . . . .

Verses

Refrain

4. May you be blessed by the Lord most high,   Ho - ly Vir - gin Ma - ry.
5. Now and for all a - ges with - out end,   Ho - ly Vir - gin Ma - ry.
6. Give praise to God in the Church and Christ,   Ho - ly Vir - gin Ma - ry.

Repeat - 'You are the honour' . . . .

THE BEATITUDES

Mt 5: 3-10, Lk 23: 43

Aideen O'Sullivan

Refrain I

D | Bm | F#m | A7

Walk in love gi - ving thanks with joy to the

G | Bm | G | Em | A | D

Fa - ther. He has called us to share his life.

Refrain II

D | F#m | G | D | A7

A - men. Tru - ly I say to you this

D | G | Em | A7 | D

day you will be with me _____ in pa - ra - dise.

Verses

D | F#m | G | Em

1. Blessed are the poor in spirit, the kingdom of
2. Blessed are the meek, for they shall in -
3. Blessed are the merciful, for they shall ob -
4. Blessed are the peacemakers, for they shall be

verses 1&3 - omit

G | A | G | G

1. heaven is theirs. Blessed are
2. - herit the earth. Blessed are those who hunger and
3. - tain mercy. Blessed are the
4. called sons of God. Blessed are those who suffer for the

A7 | D | D | E7 | A

1. those who mourn, for they shall be comforted. ℟
2. thirst for righteousness, for they shall be satisfied. ℟
3. pure in heart, for they shall see God. ℟
4. cause of right, for theirs is the kingdom of heaven. ℟

69

I AM THE BREAD OF LIFE

Text based on
Jn 6: 35, 48-54

Suzanne Toolan

Verses

1. I am the bread of life; ____ he who comes to me shall not ____
2. The bread that I will give ____ is my flesh for the life of the
3. Un - less you ____ eat ____ of the flesh of the Son of ____
4. I am the re - sur - rec - tion ____ I ____ am the ____
5. Yes Lord ____ we be - lieve ____ that ____ you ____ are the ____

1. hun - ger; he who be - lieves in me shall not thirst.
2. world ____ and he who eats ____ of this bread,
3. man ____ and ____ drink ____ of his blood and
4. life. ____ He who be - lieves ____ in me
5. Christ, ____ the ____ Son ____ of God

1. No - one can come to me ____ un - less ____ the Fa - ther draw him.
2. he shall live for - e - ver, ____ he shall live for - e - ver.
3. drink ____ of his blood, ____ you shall not have life with - in you.
4. e - ven ____ if he die ____ he shall live for - e - ver.
5. who ____ has come ____ in - to the world. ____

Refrain

And I will raise ____ him up, and I will raise ____ him

up, and I will raise ____ him up ____ on the last ____ day.

70

ALL OF MY LIFE

Text:— composite

Germaine Habjan

Refrain

All of — my life I will — sing praise to my God.

Verses

1. For cre - a -tion, —
2. For your-self, ———
3. For your grace, ———
4. To the Fa - ther, —

1. praise;	For sal - va - tion, — praise;	For all man-kind, —	praise. ℞
2. praise;	For our - selves, — sing — praise;	For each o - ther, —	praise. ℞
3. praise;	For your mer - cy, sing — praise;	For your love —	praise. ℞
4. praise;	Through the Son, — sing — praise;	In the Spi- rit,	praise. ℞

71

HEAR, O LORD

Text:— Refrain: Ray Repp
      Verses: composite

Ray Repp

Refrain

Hear, O Lord, the sound of my call. Hear, O Lord, and have

mer - cy. My soul is long - ing for the glo - ry of you. O

hear, O Lord, and an - - swer me.

Verses

1. We are but mem - bers of one house, one bro - ther -
2. We pray your life will grow in us which you a -
3. We stand a - round your al - tar, Lord to share a

1. hood we claim. Lord ac - cept this joy - ful
2. -lone can give. We pray your love will streng - then
3. com - mon meal. Our love has brought us here to -

1. praise to the glo - ry of your name. ℞
2. us; in love we wish to live. ℞
3. - day, for love makes sym - bols real. ℞

CHRIST IS OUR LORD

Pamela Stotter
based on Jean Lebon

Jean Lebon

Refrain

Christ is our Lord, he gives us life a - bun - dant.

Christ is our joy we are one in him.

Verses

1.		When the	time had	come	to re	- turn	to his
2.	That	he might	ce - le - brate	the	new	cov' - nant	with all
3.	The	cross of	Christ brings	joy	and sal	- va -	tion to
4.	While	Je - sus	slept in	death,	his dis	- ci - ples	were dis -
5.	A	stran - ger	joined two	friends	who were	talk - ing	of
6.		'Peace	be to	you',	Je - sus	said to	his dis -
7.	As -	cen - ding	to his	Fa - ther,	he	speaks	to his

1. Fa - ther	and	know - ing	that his	hour	was draw - ing
2. men.	The	Lord	gives his	bo - dy	and his
3. all.	Our	sins	he has	borne u - pon	the
4. mayed.	So	ear - ful	in their	lone - li - ness	and
5. Je - sus.	Their	hearts	burned with - in	them	as he
6. ci - ples.	'Why	are	you af - raid	and full	of
7. church.	'Pro -	claim	to all	men the	li - ving

1. near.	He longed to	share	the	Pasch	with his friends.	℟.
2. blood.	To re - con -	cile	all	men to	God once more.	℟.
3. tree.	'His death brought	life,	and	set his	peo - ple free.	℟.
4. doubt,	But he a -	rose	and	showed him - self	a - live.	℟.
5. spoke.	He broke the	bread,	they	re - cog - nized the	Lord.	℟.
6. doubt?'	With joy filled	hearts	they	gree - ted Christ,	their Lord.	℟.
7. word.'	The pro - mised	Christ	has	come to save	the world.	℟.

73

GOD IS LOVE*

Clarence Rivers

Refrain

God is love, _____ and he who ____ a - bides in
(Jn 1: 4-16)

love a - bides in God _____ and God in him. ____

Verses

1. The ___ love of Christ ___ has ___ ga - thered us to -
('Ubi Caritas' antiphon)

ge - ther. ___ Let us re - joice in him ___ and be ___ glad. ℟

2. By this shall all ___ know ___ that we ___ are his dis - ci - ples ___
(Jn 13: 35)

if we have love _____ one for a - no - ther. ℟

3. Owe ___ no ___ man _____ a - ny-thing ex - cept to love one a - no -
(Rom 13: 8-9)

*It is recommended that this song be sung unaccompanied.

74

ther, for he who loves his neigh - bour ____ will ful - fil the whole _ law. ℞

4. O ____ car - ry ____ one a - no - thers bur - dens and so you
(Gal 6: 2)

will ful - fil ____ the law of Christ. ℞ 5. The cup of bles - sing _
(1 Cor 10: 16)

____ which we bless, is it not fel-low - ship ____ in the blood of Christ? ℞

6. The ____ bread ____ which we break, ____ is ____

it not fel -low - ship ____ in ____ the bo - dy of Christ? _ ℞

7. We ma-ny are one bread, one bo - dy, for we all par -
(1 Cor 10: 17)

take of the one _ bread. ℞ 8. This is the bread that came down from
(Jn 6: 50)

hea - ven. ____ He who eats this bread shall live for e - ver. ℞

75

GIFT OF PEACE

Germaine Habjan

Refrain

G   Em   Am   D

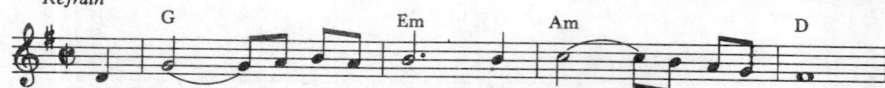

His   peace___ he gives to us,   his   peace ___ he leaves with us,

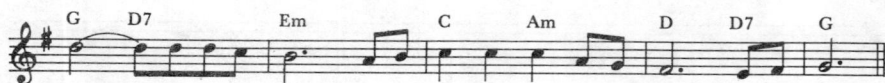

G D7   Em   C   Am   D   D7   G

not___ for us a - lone, . but that we might give it a - gain   to all men.

Verses

G   Am   D

1. The   man who looks for God   in   the   depths of his heart   will
2. The   man who sees his   life   as   an   o - pen___ door   through
3. The   man whose joy it   is   to dis - co - ver the world   and
4. The   man who knows that God has pre - pared him a home,   for

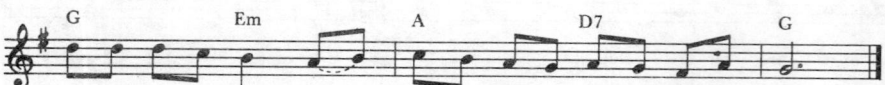

G   Em   A   D7   G

1. find a hid - den quiet that___   no - thing can dis - turb or take a - way. ℟
2. which all men might come to re - ceive and give a - gain, will know true peace. ℟
3. meet the eyes of God in the beau - ty that is his, will sing of   peace. ℟
4. all e - ter - ni - ty to re - joice and to be free, will have true peace. ℟

CHRIST IS ALIVE

Pamela Stotter   Vulpius

Verses

1. Christ is a - live, with joy we sing;   We ce - le - brate our
2. He is the grain of wheat that died,   Sown in dis - tress and
3. He is the sun which brings the dawn: He is the light of
4. He is the vine set in the earth,   Sha - ring our life, be -
5. He is the bread which comes from God,   Bro - ken to feed us
6. Christ is a - live, with joy we sing;   We ce - le - brate our

1. ri - sen Lord, Prai - sing the glo - ry of his name. ℟
2. reaped in joy, Yiel - ding a har - vest of new life. ℟
3. all the world, Set - ting us free from death and sin. ℟
4. - co - ming man, That man might share in God's own life. ℟
5. in our need, Gi - ven to bring e - ter - nal life. ℟
6. ri - sen Lord, Prai - sing the glo - ry of his name. ℟

Refrain

Al - le - lu - ia, _____ Al - le - lu - ia, _____ Al - le - lu - ia.

RENEW YOUR HEARTS

Text:— composite   Jean Paul Lécot

Re - new your hearts, re - pent and be - lieve in the Gos -

pel. Re - turn to God, for he is rich in mer - cy.

Verses

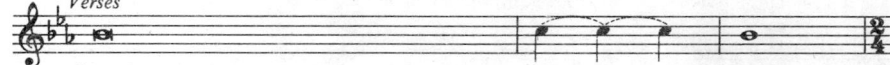

1. I do not come to con - demn __ the world.
2. I do not come for those who are heal - thy or just.
3. I do not come to judge _____ anyone.
4. I am the good _____ shepherd.
5. I am the gate of the sheepfold.
6. He who believes has e - ter - nal life.

1. I come to bring sal - va - tion to all men. ℟
2. I come to help the weak and those in sin. ℟
3. I come to give all men e - ter - nal life. ℟
4. I come to give my life __ for the sheep. ℟
5. The man who en - ters by me will be saved. ℟
6. My words to you are spi - rit, they are life. ℟

77

UNLESS A MAN IS BORN FROM ABOVE

Text based on Jn 3

Gregory Norbert O.S.B.

Verse

1. O Fa - ther, we are in your hands. Give us your Spi - rit

that we may live what we pro - claim.

Refrain

Un - less a man is born from a - bove

he can - not see the king - dom of God.

2. Unless a man is born through wa - ter and the Spi - rit, he cannot enter the

king-dom of God. What is born of the flesh is flesh. What is born of the

Spi - rit is Spi - rit. ℟ 3. The wind blows where - e - ver it plea-ses.

You hear its sound, but you cannot tell where it comes from, or where it is go - ing.

This is how it is with all who are born of the Spi - rit. ℟

THOUGH SO MANY WE ARE ONE

Text - composite

Jean Paul Lécot

Refrain

Though so many we are one sharing in the holy Bread of Life. We are the Body of Jesus Christ the Lord. We gather in his name.

Verses

1. I am the living bread which came down from heaven.
2. On the night when he was be-trayed,
3. Taking the cup, he gave thanks and praise;
4. One in the Spirit, we share God's life;
5. As we eat this bread, may we grow in love;
6. Give praise to the Father for his steadfast love,

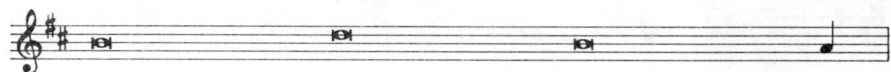

1. He who eats of this bread lives for- ever
2. To show his friends the depths of his love
3. He shared it with all his dis- ciples, and said,
4. One in our faith, we ac- claim one Lord;
5. May our lives be a sacrifice of praise.
6. Through his Son, Jesus Christ, who freed us from death,

1. The bread that I will give to you.
2. Jesus took bread, gave thanks and said,
3. 'Take and drink the cup of my blood,
4. One body in Christ we share one bread
5. May we share each other's burdens and joys,
6. In the Holy Spirit sing praise to God

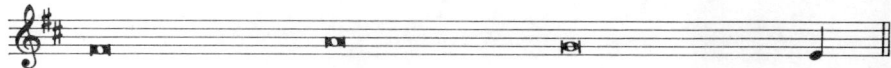

1. Is my flesh for the life of the world ℞
2. 'This is my body, given for you'. ℞
3. shed for you, and for all man- kind'. ℞
4. One heart in love we drink from one cup. ℞
5. living not for our- selves, but for Christ the Lord. ℞
6. Now and for- ever and ever, A- men. ℞

79

WHEN THE TIME CAME TO STRETCH OUT HIS ARMS

Text:— composite

Jo Akepsimas

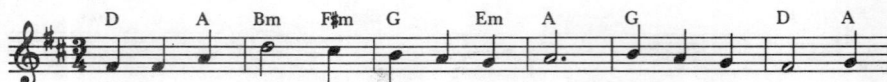

1. When the time came to stretch out his arms, And to lay down his
2. This is my flesh, O take it and eat. This is my blood, O
3. Hun - ger and thirst no lon - ger we fear, Christ's ho - ly flesh be -
4. O bread of life, O Ban - quet Di - vine, Sign of the love that
5. Through Je - sus Christ, the per - fect high Priest, And in the Spi - rit

1. life for his friends God's on - ly Son in the brea-king of bread, Gave his own
2. take it and drink, And to pro - claim my__ death for man - kind, This must you
3.-comes now our food. And when we raise his__ cha - lice to drink, Joy o - ver -
4. makes us all one. We who now share this__ gift from a - bove, Sure - ly have
5. source of our peace. For this great feast which__ you have pre - pared, Fa - ther a -

1. flesh as food for man - kind, Gave his own flesh as food for man - kind.
2. do, Un - til I re - turn, This must you do un - til I re - turn.
3. flows, Our hope is re - newed, Joy o - ver - flows, our hope is re - newed.
4. seen the good-ness of God, Sure - ly have seen the good-ness of God.
5. -bove, O praised be your name, Fa - ther a - bove, O praised be your name.

80

CHRIST OUR LORD HAS COME TO SAVE HIS PEOPLE

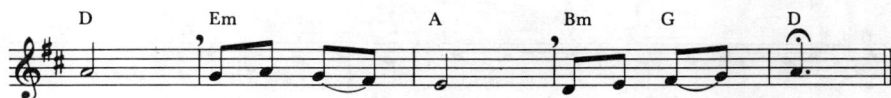

Sr Lucia

Paul Décha

Refrain

Christ, our Lord has come to save his peo - ple Al - le - lu —
ia. Al - le - lu - ia. Al - le - lu - ia.

Verses

1. We are bap - tised in Christ, re - born to new life in our
2. O come, bless our God the Fa - ther of all who is
3. From all e - ter - ni - ty he loved us and planned to a -
4. Be joy - ful in the Lord, re - joice and give thanks to the
5. With Christ we are made heirs and called to be - long to the
6. Give glo - ry to God the Fa - ther of all, to his

1. Sa - viour and Lord, Al - le - lu - ia. For we are the peo - ple whom
2. love with - out end, Al - le - lu - ia. Be - fore he cre - a - ted the
3. dopt - us in Christ, Al - le - lu - ia. He chose us to live in his
4. Fa - ther of all, Al - le - lu - ia. For Christ is a - live and we
5. fa - mi - ly of God, Al - le - lu - ia. Christ freed us from sin by his
6. Son Je - sus Christ, Al - le - lu - ia. And praise to the Spi - rit, the

1. God made his own through the blood of his Son, our Lord Je - sus Christ. ℟
2. world with great power, he chose us in Christ, and made us his own. ℟
3. glo - ri - ous name as his chil - dren and friends, a peo - ple re - deemed. ℟
4. live now in him; we are filled with his power, re - joice, praise his name. ℟
5. death on the cross, and raised us to life, a life with - out end. ℟
6. gift of love, let us sing to the Lord, for - e - ver, A - men. ℟

81

THE LORD JESUS

Text based on Jn 13

Gregory Norbert O.S.B.

Refrain

B7   E   C#m   F#m   B7   E

The Lord — Je - sus, af- ter ea-ting with his friends, washed their

A   E   A

feet and said to them, 'Do you know what I, your Lord, have done to

F#m   B7   E   C#m

you?_____ I have gi - ven you ex - am - ple,___

F#m   B7   E

that so you al - so should do'. _____

Verses

E   C#m   A   B7

1. You— are my friends; a man can have no grea - ter love than to
2. Peace I leave with you, my peace I give to all who live with
3. I___ am the vine and you the branch, re - main in me and
4. He who comes to me will ne - ver thirst, nor want for food and

C#m   F#m   B

1. give his life ____ for ____ his friends. _____ ℞
2. bound - less love for all ____ man - kind. _____ ℞
3. you will bear a - bun - dant fruit. _____ ℞
4. I will raise him up on the last day. _____ ℞

82

DONA NOBIS PACEM

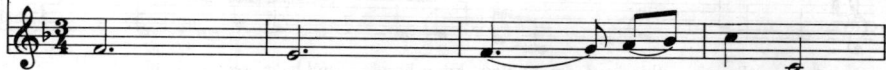

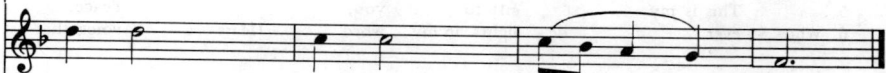

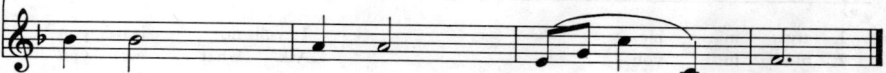

Anon

Do - na no - bis pa - cem, pa - cem:

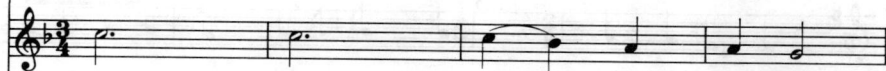

Do - na no - bis pa - cem,

Do - na no - bis pa - cem,

Do - na no - bis pa - cem.

Do - na no - bis pa - cem.

Do - na no - bis pa - cem.

I AM THE WAY

Text based on
Jn 14: 6

Aideen O'Sullivan

Refrain

I am the way, the truth and the life. No one can come to the

Fa ther ex- cept through me. If you know me, you know my Fa-ther

too. From this mo - ment you know him, and have seen — him.

Verses

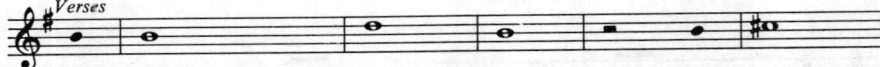

1.	Do not let your	hearts be	troubled.	Trust in	God still and
2.	If you a -	bide in	me	And my	words a -
3. By	this is my	Father	glorified,		That you
4.	As the	Father has	loved me,	so	I have
5.	This is my	gift to	you,		Peace,
6. Who - ever		de - lights in my	word	Hears a	voice that

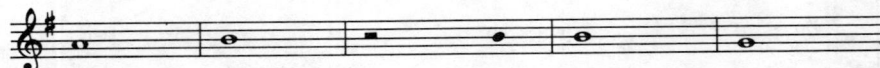

1. trust in	me.		I will not	leave you	
2. bide in	you,		Ask what -	ever you	
3. bear much	fruit.	Who -	ever a -	bides in	
4. loved	you.		Love each	other from the	
5. not of this	world.	May	peace	dwell in your	
6. speaks of	peace.	Fill your	minds with	what is	

1. desolate.		I will re -	turn	to	you. ℟
2. will	And	it shall be	done	for	you. ℟
3. me,	Will	bear a - bun -	dant	fruit. ℟	
4. heart,	That your	joy	may	be	full. ℟
5. hearts,		Peace	in	your	homes. ℟
6. good,	And the	God of	peace will	be	with you. ℟

84

YOU ARE MY SERVANT

Text based on Is 41-43

Aideen O'Sullivan

Refrain

You are my ser - vant, I have cho - sen you, and not cast you off. Do not fear for I am with you.

Verses

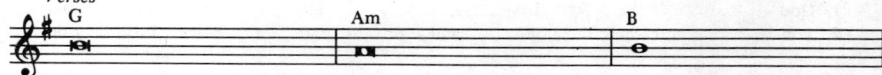

1. Be not dismayed for I am your God.
2. Fear not, for I have re - deemed you.
3. You are a covenant to the peoples,
4. I, the Lord your God hold your right hand.
5. You shall re - joice in the Lord.
6. I, the Lord will answer you.

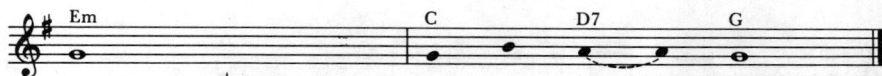

1. I will strengthen you, I will help ____ you. ℟
2. I have called your name, you are mine. ____ ℟
3. A light to the na - tions. ℟
4. It is I who say to you 'I am with ____ you'. ℟
5. And glory in the Ho - ly one of Israel. ℟
6. I, the God of Israel will not for - sake ____ you. ℟

85

LET NOT YOUR HEARTS BE TROUBLED

Jn 14: 1-13

Anon

1. Let not your hearts be — trou - bled, you be - lieve — in
2. I go to pre - pare — a — place — for

1. God be - lieve _____ al - so in me. __
2. you, and when I go and pre - pare a place for you, —

1. __ In my Fa - ther's house are ma - ny man -
2. I will come a - gain and take __ you to my -

1. - sions, if it were not so, would I have told — you? ___
2. - self, that where I am, there you may be al - so. _____

86

STEADFAST LOVE

Is 60: 19, 54: 7-10

Aideen O' Sullivan

Refrain I

Em | Am Em | Am | Em

No more will the sun give you day - light, nor moon-light shine on you, but

C | G | Am | Em Em7 | A

Yah - weh will be your e - ver - las-ting light, your God will be your splen - dour.

Verses

Em | Am

1. With love e - ver - las - ting____ I have loved__ you,
3. Once more there shall be poured out the Spi - rit from a - bove.

Em | Bm | Am | Bm

1. there - fore I have drawn__ you, in pi - ty looked on you.
3. Then__ shall the wil - der - ness be - come a fer - tile land.

Refrain II

Em | Am | Bm | C

R. 2. 'For the moun-tains may de - part, and the hills be re - moved, but my

Am | D | Am | Am | D

stead- fast love will not de - part from you, and my co - ve- nant of peace will

Em | Am | Bm C | D G | D

not be re- moved' says the Lord, who has com - pas - sion on you.

Em *Verses* | Am

2. Lis - ten, pay at - ten - tion and your soul will live.
4. Yah - weh, you give peace, we place our trust in you.

Em | Bm | Am | D

2. Seek Yah - weh, call__ him__ while he is still near.____ R/I
4. Our e - ver - las - ting rock, we hope in you for - e - ver. R/I

87

GLORY OF CREATION

Pamela Stotter   Wachet Auf

1. Day and night the heav'ns are tel - ling The glo - ry which with
   Dawn and dusk are still with won - der. The wind cries out, the

2. Lord, we stand in awe be - fore you, Your peo - ple co - ming
   See us now in sha - dows dwel - ling, And come like sun, the

1. us is dwel - ling, The works of God to us made known
   wa - ters thun - der, Dis - play - ing his al - migh - ty power.

2. to a - dore you, So cleanse our hearts, re - new our minds.
   clouds dis - pel - ling, En - ligh - ten, heal us, Lord of love.

1. Our God is great in - deed. He knows our con - stant
2. Your Spi - rit in us prays. He tea - ches us your

1. need, our cre - a - tor. So with cre - a - tion
2. ways, as we li - sten. Touch once a - gain with

1. we pro - claim his good - ness as we praise his name.
2. li - ving flame your peo - ple ga - thered in your name.

88

GIFT OF FINEST WHEAT

Omer Westendorf

Robert E. Kreutz

Refrain

You sa-tis-fy the hun-gry heart — with gift of fi-nest wheat; Come give to us, O— sa-ving Lord, The bread of life to eat.—

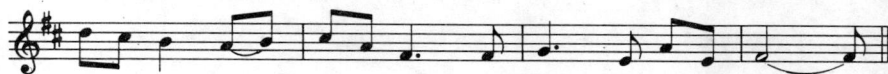

Verses

1. As when the shep-herd calls his sheep, They know and heed his voice; So
2. With joy-ful lips we sing to you Our praise and gra-ti-tude, That
3. Is not the cup we bless and share The blood of Christ out-poured? Do
4. The mys-t'ry of your pre-sence, Lord, No mor-tal tongue can tell: Whom
5. You give your-self to us, O Lord: Then self-less let us be, To

1. when you call your fam-'ly, Lord we fol-low and re-joice. ℟
2. you should count us wor-thy, Lord, To share this heav'n-ly food. ℟
3. not one cup, one loaf, de-clare Our one-ness in the Lord? ℟
4. all the world can-not con-tain Comes in our hearts to dwell. ℟
5. serve each o-ther in your name In truth and cha-ri-ty. ℟

89

MORNING HAS BROKEN

Eleanor Farjeon   Bunessan

1. Mor-ning has bro - ken like the first mor - ning, black-bird has
2. Sweet the rain's new fall sun - lit from hea - ven, like the first
· 3. Mine is the sun - light, mine is the mor - ning, born of the

1. spo - ken, like the first bird. Praise for the sing - ing! Praise for the
2. dew fall on the first grass. Praise for the sweet - ness of the wet
3. one light E - den saw play! Praise with e - la - tion praise ev' - ry

1. mor - ning: Praise for them spring - ing fresh from the Word.
2. gar - den, sprung in com - plete - ness where his feet pass.
3. mor - ning, God's re - cre - a - tion of the new day.

Alternative words to this melody:

1. This day God gives me
    Strength of high heaven,
    Sun and moon shining,
    Flame in my hearth,
    Flashing of lightning,
    Wind in its swiftness,
    Deeps of the ocean,
    Firmness of earth.

2. This day God sends me
    Strength as my steersman
    Might to uphold me,
    Wisdom as guide.
    Your eyes are watchful,
    Your ears are listening,
    Your lips are speaking,
    Friend at my side.

3. God's way is my way,
    God's shield is round me,
    God's host defends me,
    Saving from ill.
    Angels of heaven
    Drive from me always
    All that would harm me,
    Stand by me still.

4. Rising, I thank you,
    Mighty and strong one,
    King of creation,
    Giver of rest,
    Firmly confessing
    Threeness of persons,
    Oneness of Godhead,
    Trinity blest.

Adapted from "St Patrick's Breastplate" by James Quinn S.J.

90

I SEARCH EVERYWHERE FOR THE
FACE OF THE LORD

Translation composite
Refrain

Text and Music
Odette Vercruysse

I search — eve-ry-where — for the face — of the Lord, — I

seek — his re - flec - tion — in the depths — of your hearts.

Verses

You are — the Bo-dy of Christ. — You are — the

Blood of Christ. — You are — the (1) love of Christ. — Why
(2) joy
(3) peace

then — have you for - sa - ken him? — ℞

The song may be repeated, substituting the words
'joy' and 'peace' as indicated at bar 14.

DAY BY DAY

D. Austin

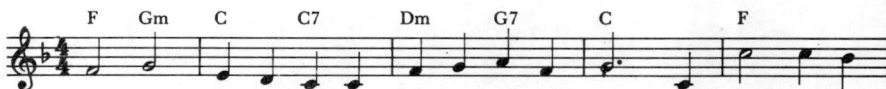

Day by day, dear Lord, of thee three things I pray; to see thee more

clear-ly, to love thee more dear - ly to fol - low thee more near- ly, day · by day.

91

COME, O LORD

Roger Ruston

Early American Folk Song

Verses

1. Pro - mised Lord and Christ — is he
2. Tea - ching, hea - ling once__ was he
3. Dead and bu - ried once__ was he
4. Ri - sen from the dead__ is he
5. Soon to come a - gain__ is he

1-5. May we soon his king - dom see.

Refrain

Come, O Lord, quick - ly__ come. Come in glo - ry,

come in glo - ry, come_ in glo - ry, quick - ly__ come.

92

WHERE THERE IS CHARITY AND LOVE

Text based on 'Ubi Caritas'

Richard Connolly

Refrain

Where there is cha - ri - ty and love, there ___ the

God of love ___ a - bides. ___

1st and last times | **before verses**

Verses

1. The love of Christ has ga - thered us as one; ___
2. And so when we are ga - thered here as one, ___
3. O lead us, Mas - ter by ___ your sa - ving grace ___

1. Re - joice ___ in him with joy which he ___ im - parts. ___
2. Let quar - rels die and en - vious ran - cour cease. ___
3. To where ___ the bless - ed glo - ry in ___ your sight. ___

1. ___ Let us re - vere and love ___ the li - ving God, ___
2. ___ Be our re - solve all bit - ter - ness ___ to shun. ___
3. ___ There let us see and love ___ you face ___ to face, ___

1. ___ And love each o - ther with ___ un - feign - ing hearts. ___ ℟
2. ___ And in our midst be Christ, ___ his love ___ and peace. ___ ℟
3. ___ · Ga-thered once more in e - ver - last - ing light. ___ ℟

93

THE SPIRIT OF THE LORD

Text:— composite   Traditional Dutch Melody

1. The Spi - rit of the Lord re - news his church in
2. He is the power of God who o'er cre - a - tion
3. And he who lives in us begs God with ev' - ry

1. love. The pro - mise now_ ful - filled, he tea - ches us_ of
2. broods, and draws all things to Christ, in whom they find_ their
3. breath to make us, in _ the Son rise up now from_ the

1. God. The _ Fa - ther's gift to _ us, who brings his hea - ling
2. life. In _ him we are bap - tized, a - noin - ted with his
3. dead. The _ Spi - rit and the_ bride say 'Come, O Christ the

1. power The bro - ken he re - stores the woun - ded he _ makes whole.
2. seal, to be, through bro - ken bread the bo - dy of _ the Lord.
3. Lord', that in him who is Lord, God may be all _ in all.

YAHWEH

Gregory Norbert O.S.B.   Gregory Norbert O.S.B.

Refrain

E   A   E   C#m   A

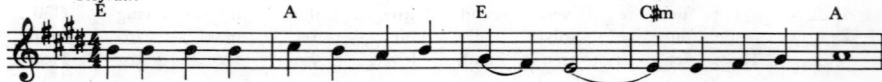

Yah - weh is the God of my sal - va - tion_____ I trust in him

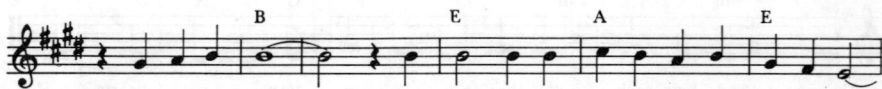

B   E   A   E

and have no fear._ I sing of the joy which his love gives to me_

C m   A   B7   E

_ and I draw deep - ly from the springs of his great kind - ness._

94

E   G m   A   B

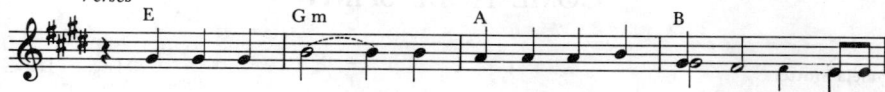

1. O - pen our eyes to the won - der of this mo - ment, the be-
2. When eve - ning comes and our day of toil is o - ver, give us
3. Take us be - yond the vi - sion of this day to the

C#m   A   F m   B

1. - gin - ning of a - no - ther day. _____ ℟
2. rest, __ O Lord in the joy of ma - ny friends. _____ ℟
3. deep and wide ways of your in - fi - nite love and life. _____ ℟

MAY CHRIST LIVE IN OUR HEARTS

Text adapted from   Suzanne Toolan
Eph 2: 21, 3: 17

Verses   F   C   F7   Bb   Gm

1. May __ Christ __ live in our hearts, __ through faith may he be with
2. For __ this we pray to the Fa - ther, that __ he may __ give us
3. With __ cou - rage then in our prayer, __ we ap - proach the __ Lord in
4. May we stand __ firm in the truth, __ hold __ fast the __ shield of

C   C7   Dm   Gm   Am   Dm   Gm   G7   C

1. us, that __ plan - ted and built on love, we may pro - claim his good-ness.
2. power, in his Spi - rit __ that we may grow in love and in - ner strength. _
3. trust, for __ we _____ are God's work, a tem - ple to his glo - ry.
4. faith, pro - claim the __ gos - pel of peace, in ea - ger ho - nest deeds. _

Refrain   F   Bb   F   F7   Bb

Glo - ry be to __ him whose power is at work in us.

Am   Dm   Gm   C7   F

Praise God the Fa - ther of our Lord Je - sus Christ.

COME HOLY SPIRIT

Pamela Stotter

Margaret Daly
(Veni Creator)

Refrain

Come, Ho - ly Spi - rit, Al - le - lu - ia. Come, grea-test gift of God,

Al - le - lu - ia. Come, re - new the___ face___ of the earth.

Verses

1. Fill our hearts with the light of your spi - rit, And
2. God the Fa - ther___ sends the___ spi - rit To
3. By his power we ac - claim Je - sus Christ as Lord, For
4. In the free - dom___ of the___ spi - rit, we
5. By our sha - ring in God's own___ spi - rit, He

1. kin dle in us the fire___ of your love. May we___ wor-ship you in
2. bring to___ mind the words of the Lord; 'Peace I___ leave with you, my
3. us he___ died and rose a - gain. Now in___ glo - ry at
4. learn to___ pray as sons___ of___ God; 'Ab - ba___ Fa - ther', we
5. lives in___ us, and we___ in___ him. 'Love each___ o - ther as

1. spi - rit and___ truth; May your___ praise bring joy to our lives. ℟
2. own___ peace I give, Re - ceive my___ spi - rit, gift of___ peace'. ℟
3. God's___ right___ hand, He sends his___ spi - rit to the___ Church. ℟
4. cry___ to___ him; The spi - rit___ prays with in our___ hearts. ℟
5. God___ loves___ you, And so ful - fil the law of ___ ' Christ'. ℟

96

COME TO ME

Mk 11: 28-30

Gregory Norbert O.S.B.

Refrain

Come to me all who la - bour and are hea - vy bur - dened and I shall give you rest. Take up my yoke and learn from me for I am meek and hum - ble of heart and you'll find rest for your souls. Yes my yoke is ea - sy, and my bur - den is light.

Verse

The Lord is my shep - herd, I shall ne - ver be in need; fresh and green are the mea - dows where he gives me rest. Come to

D.C. al Fine

97

BRING BREAD

Jucunda Laudatio

Gregory Murray O.S.B.

Verses

1. Reap me the earth as a har - vest to God, ga - ther and bring it a - gain,
2. Go with your song and your mu - sic, with joy, go to the al - tar of God.
3. Glad - ness and pi - ty and pas - sion and pain all that is mor - tal in man,

1. all that is his to the ma - ker of all. Lift it and of - fer it high.
2. Car - ry your of - fe - rings, fruits of the earth, work of your la - bou-ring hands.
3. lay all be-fore him, re - turn him his gift, God to whom all shall go home.

Refrain

Bring bread, bring wine, give glo - ry to the Lord.

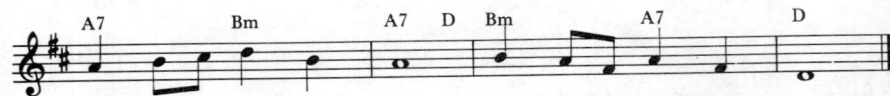

Whose is the earth but God's? Whose is the praise but his?

PRAYER OF ST FRANCIS

Donovan

1. Make me an in - stru - ment of your peace.
2. Where there is in - ju - ry let me sow par - don.

1. Where there is ha tred let me sow love.
2. Where there is doubt let me sow faith.

It is in

98

(music)

gi - ving that we — re - ceive.— It is in par - do - ning

that we are par - doned. It is in dy - ing that we — are

born, that we are born, to e - ter - nal life.

O WITH WHAT JOY WE SING OF MARY

Gregory Norbert O.S.B.

(music: G Em C G)

O with what joy we sing of Ma - ry, a wo - man of great love,

(music: G Em C G)

whose o - pen - ness and lo - ving kind - ness gave birth to God's own Son.

(music: G Am G C D)

Ma - ry, O so gen - tle and dis - creet, be with us as we pray

(music: G Em C Am G)

to know the whis - per of his pre - sence, the won - der of his love.

LET ALL WHO ARE BAPTISED WALK IN THE LIGHT OF CHRIST

Text by J.P. Lecot
Translated by Sr Mary Lucia

Paul Décha

Refrain

Let all who are bap-tised walk in the light of Christ for
he is our Ri-sen Lord, al-le-lu - ia, al-le-lu - ia.

Verses

1. We pro-claim that the Lord is kind and lo - ving, his stead-fast
2. To all those who were sor-row-ful and wea - ry, or who were
3. Let us tell of the mer-cy of our Fa - ther, to those who
4. Those who cry to the Lord in their af-flic - tion, and all who
5. The Lord heals the sad and the low - ly, those o-ver
6. Let us give thanks and praise to God our Fa - ther, and to his

1. love lasts for a-ges un-en-ding. Let his peo-ple announce to all the
2. ex-iled in pain or in sad-ness, He has gi-ven his com-fort and his
3. know fear and pain thirst and hun-ger, He has shown the great power of his right
4. call on his love and his mer-cy Will be res-cued from dark-ness and from
5. whelmed by their sins and of-fen-ses. He gives 'life to the peo-ple who re-
6. son Je-sus Christ, our Re-dee-mer, To the Spi-rit who lives with-in our

1. world That he saves and brings all man-kind to - ge - ther. ℟
2. help He has led them in-to a land of plen - ty. ℟
3. hand, It is he who pro-tects his faith-ful peo - ple. ℟
4. death Will be freed from the chains of sin and blind - ness. ℟
5. pent And his life - gi-ving word re-vives their spi - rit. ℟
6. hearts, At all times, in all pla-ces and for - e - ver. ℟

100

FILL US WITH YOUR PRAISE

Text based on
Ps 70: 8,23

Mary Mc Cooey

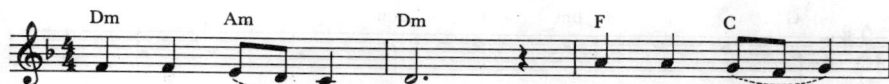

1. Fill us with your praise. Fill us with your
2. Al - le - lu - ia, al - le - lu -

praise,___ and we will sing___ your_ glo - ry.
ia,___ al - le - lu - ia, al - le - lu - ia,

Songs of joy___ will be e - ver on our lips.
Songs of joy___ will be e - ver on our lips.

This hymn may be repeated substituting 'love', 'peace', 'joy', for 'praise.'

SINLESS MAIDEN

M.K. Richardson

Melody from
Arbeau's Orchésographie

1. Sin - less mai - den, low - ly Ma - ry of
2. Hap - py Mo - ther, low - ly Ma - ry of
3. Va - liant wo - man, low - ly Ma - ry on

1. Ga - li - lee, Ga - bri - el now
2. Beth - le - hem. Shep - herds star - ward
3. Cal - va - ry, Stan - ding by her

1. asks you Mo - ther of God ____ to be.
2. ga - zing, Ma - gi join ____ with them.
3. Son's cross, all ____ the world ____ can see.

HAIL MARY

Clarence Rivers

Hail__ Ma - ry full of grace the __ Lord is __ with__

thee Bles - sed art thou a - mong wo - men, and bles - sed

is the fruit of thy womb, Je - sus. Ho - ly Ma - ry,

Mo-ther of God __ pray for us sin - ners now and at the

hour__ of our death. A - men, A - men,__ A - men.

FOR YOU SHALL GO OUT IN JOY

Text based on
Is 55:12, Zeph 3:14-18, Ps 71

Aideen O'Sullivan

Refrain

For you shall go out in joy and be led forth in peace. The
moun-tains and the hills be - fore you break forth in - to
song, And all the trees of the field shall clap their
hands, And all the trees of the field shall clap their hands.

Verses

1. ⁷ Je - ru - sa - lem, a - rise, _____ stand_ on the heights, And
2. Let the moun - tains and hills bring a mes - sage __ of peace To
3. All the ends of the earth __ will see the power of God. The
4. Sing a - loud Is - ra - el, _____ re joice with all your heart, The
5. Let the hea - vens be glad, _____ let all the earth re - joice, The

1. see the joy that comes to you from God. Rise and clothe your-self in strength.
2. all __ who are wai-ting for the Lord. May he come to those in need.
3. Lord_ will make known his sal - va - tion. Let the ri - vers clap their hands
4. Lord_ your God is in your midst. No more e - vil will you fear
5. sea and all with-in it thun-der praise. Let the fields ex-ult with joy,

1. Show your splen-dour to the world For the Lord_ has__ com-for - ted his peo - ple. ℞
2. May his hea - ling bring them joy For their lives _ are __ pre-cious in his sight. ℞
3. Let the hills ring out their joy For the Lord_comes to rule _____ the earth. ℞
4. No more will you stand a - lone For the Lord _ will re-new you in his love. ℞
5. All the wood-land trees re-joice At the pre-sence of the Lord,_ for he comes. ℞

LET US WELCOME THE LORD

Pamela Stotter

Jean Paul Lécot

Refrain

Let us wel - come the Lord . for he comes, and all men will see the sal - va - tion of our God.

Verses

1.	All cre - a - tion longs	for	the	co - ming	of	the	Sa - viour,	As
2.	By his sear-ching light	he	will	scat - ter	all	our	sha - dows,	And
3.	He who has this hope	has		placed	all	his	trust in God,	For
4.	We shall know God's peace	.at	the	co - ming	of	our	sa - viour.	The
5.	Walk-ing in his light,	we		sing our	song	of	wel - come,	The

1.	watch - men	wait	for	the	co - ming	dawn.	The
2.	heal	our	hearts	of	the	wounds of	sin.	Our
3.	God	will be	faith -	ful	to	all	his	word.	He
4.	world	shall be	filled	with	the	glo - ry	of	God.	His
5.	song	of the	bride,	"Ma - ra - na	-	tha!"	So

1.	Ri - sing	Sun	ap - pears	and	sheds	his	light. R.
2.	sa - viour	and	our	Lord	will	give	us	hope. R.
3.	comes	in	love	and	peace	to	dwell	with	us. R.
4.	faith - ful - ness	and	love	will	be	re -	vealed. R.
5.	quick - ly	come,	Lord	Je -	sus,	A -	men! R.

105

SPRING OF NEW HOPE

Pamela Stotter   Tamié

Cantor

Like ri - vers in the de - sert, like springs from the rock,

new hope came through Ma - ry, when the Word be - came

flesh and our hu - man - i - ty re -gained its for - mer glo - ry

Refrain

Bles -sed Ma - ry, spring of new hope, from your son flow the wa - ters of life

Verses

1. The song of the spring will glo - ri - fy the Lord. R.

2. The fresh - ness of the clear cool - ing spring will quench our burn - ing thirst. R.

3. This ri - ver in our de - sert will fill our hearts with joy. R.

cantor repeats — Like rivers in the desert . . . All repeat *Refrain*

SURELY HE HAS BORNE OUR GRIEFS

Text based on Is 53

Aideen O'Sullivan

Refrain

Sure-ly he has borne our griefs and car - ried our sor - rows

Yet we es-teemed him stric - ken, smit - ten by God and af - flic ted.

Verses

1. He was bruised for our in - iquities
   His punishment brought us peace,
2. He was rejected and des - pised by men,
   The Lord burdened him with our sins,
3. He was like a lamb led to slaughter
   Harshly dealt with, he bore it humbly,
4. He shall see the fruit of his suffering
   By his suffering, my servant shall jus - ti - fy many,

1. He was crushed for our sins.
   Through his wounds we are healed. ℟.
2. A man of sorrows and ac - quain ted with grief.
   In silence he bowed to the stroke. ℟.
3. He was torn from the land of the living.
   Though he had done no wrong. ℟.
4. His soul shall be satisfied
   Taking their sins on him self. ℟.

SONG OF THE BANQUET

Pamela Stotter
based on Claude Duchesneau

Claude Duchesneau

Cantor

1. Who wel - comes us to come to him and share his bread?
2. You lead us to your ta - ble, Lord, that we may eat,
3. O Lord, u - nite our lives with yours as gifts of love
4. O God of power and might, we wor - ship you in song,
5. With you, O Lord we eat this bread and drink this wine
6. So great your love, you coun - ted ev - 'ry thing but loss.

All

1. WHO FILLS THE CUP WHICH O - VER - FLOWS WITH WINE SO RED?
2. AND THOSE WHO FOL - LOW YOU WILL FIND THEIR JOY COM - PLETE.
3. THAT WE MAY JOIN CRE - A - TION'S SONG TO GOD A - BOVE.
4. THE GOD OF HO - LI - NESS TO WHOM WE NOW BE - LONG.
5. AS WE RE - CALL YOUR SA - CRI - FICE BY THIS GREAT SIGN.
6. TO SHOW YOUR LOVE YOU DIED FOR US U - PON A CROSS.

Cantor

1. Who called and brought us to - ge - ther here?
2. Your life grows in us like wheat and vine.
3. May joy - ful sing - ing like in - cense rise.
4. As once you spoke and your word brought life,
5. By dy - ing you showed us how to give.
6. 'O death your sting is des - troyed', we cry

All

1. WHO GIVES US JOY WHEN HE DRAWS US NEAR?
2. YOUR LIFE SUS - TAINS US WITH BREAD AND WINE.
3. WITH PRAISE WE OF - FER OUR SA - CRI - FICE.
4. SO NOW YOU HEAL ALL OUR PAIN AND STRIFE.
5. BY RI - SING YOU GAVE US LIFE TO LIVE.
6. 'O GRAVE, YOUR VIC - TO - RY WE DE - NY'.

1. My friends, come to the feast and we shall know his name.
2. Our hearts, bur - ning with love re - joice to hear you call.
3. By you we are made one in spi - rit and in mind.
4. Come speak now to our hearts; we know your word is true.
5. With joy, we ce - le - brate your pre - sence with us here.
6. For Christ, Sa - viour and Lord has ri - sen from the dead.

All

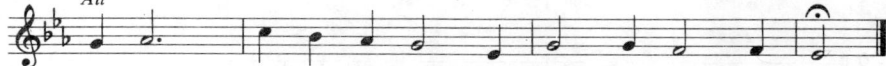

1. O COME, JOIN IN THE FEAST, HIS LOVE WE SHALL PRO – CLAIM.
2. BY FAITH WE SEE AND KNOW THAT YOU ARE LORD OF ALL.
3. THROUGH YOU PEACE IS RE–STORED WITH GOD AND WITH MAN - KIND.
4. O COME, LORD JE - SUS CHRIST, WE WAIT IN HOPE FOR YOU.
5. WITH HOPE, WAI - TING FOR YOU IN GLO - RY TO AP - PEAR.
6. HE LIVES, DWEL-LING IN US, AND FEEDS US WITH HIS BREAD.

O COMFORT MY PEOPLE

Chrysogonus Waddell
based on Is 40

Gaelic

1. O__ com - fort my__ peo - ple and __ calm all their__ fear, And
2. Pro - claim to the__ ci - ties of__ Ju - da my __ word: That
3. All __ moun-tains and__ hills shall be - come as a ___ plain For

1. tell them the__ time__ of sal - va - tion__ draws_ near. O
2. gen - tle yet__ strong_ is the__ hand of__ the__ Lord. I
3. van - ished are__ mour - ning and__ hun - ger__ and__ pain. And

1. tell them_ I___ come_ to re - move all __ their__ shame. Then__
2. res - cue___ the__ cap - tives my__ peo - ple__ de - fend. And__
3. ne - ver a - gain shall these war a - gainst you. Be -

1. they will for - e - ver give ___ praise to my name.
2. bring them to __ jus - tice and___ joy with - out end.
3. hold I come_ quick - ly to____ make all things new.

109

ARISE, JERUSALEM

Pamela Stotter
based on Jean Debruynne

Gaëtan de Courrèges

Verses

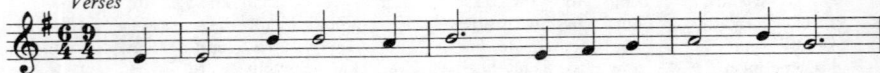

1. A - rise, Je - ru - sa - lem, ci - ty of God our Sa -
2. A - rise, Je - ru - sa - lem, ci - ty who stoned the pro -
3. A - rise, Je - ru - sa - lem, come all you men and wo -

1. viour, _____ for now the time has come to robe your -
2. phets. _____ You sang no song of tears when men of
3. men, _____ The pro - mised time has come. Here God has

1. self in splen - dour. _____ Come forth, dressed in fine
2. vi - sion left you. _____ Your bread lost its good
3. made his dwel - ling. _____ And you, chil - dren of

1. gold, _____ your crown shi - ning like sun - beams, _____ put
2. taste, _____ your wine gave you no plea - sure. _____ Re -
3. light, _____ must leave all that is dark - ness. _____ A -

1. on your cloak of peace, ga - ther the poor be - neath its folds. _____
2. pent of all your sin. God will re - store your glo - ry. _____
3. rise, your light has come. Shout out your cry of glad - ness. _____

Refrain

1. PUT ON YOUR CLOAK OF PEACE, GA - THER THE POOR BE - NEATH ITS FOLDS.
2. RE - PENT OF ALL YOUR SIN, GOD WILL RE - STORE YOUR GLO - RY.
3. A - RISE YOUR LIGHT HAS COME. SHOUT OUT YOUR SONG OF GLAD - NESS.

110

HYMN TO LOVE

Pamela Stotter
based on 1 Cor 13

David Julien

Refrain

The gifts of God poured out on his church are faith hope and love and the grea-test of all is the gift of love.

Verses

1. For love shows great pa-tience, and love meets all needs and ne-ver en-vies o-thers,— al-ways be-ing kind, al-ways gen-tle, al-ways true. ℟.

2. And love is not sel-fish. Love is ne-ver rude, but love brings for-give-ness. Peace sure-ly dwells in the hearts of those who love. ℟.

3. And love looks for truth, con-demn-ing all in-jus-tice, up-hol-ding what is right. Love will stand firm and love will o-ver-come. ℟.

4. Love is filled with hope, and love be-lieves all things for love en-dures when all else fails. ℟.

GLORY BE TO YOU

Pamela Stotter
based on C.F.C.

Joseph Gelineau

Cantor

1. God most high of all cre - a - tion, Glo - ry be to you!
2. God of light, our dark - ness end - ing, Glo - ry be to you!
3. Migh - ty God who brings us free - dom, Glo - ry be to you!
4. God of love, your ways are gen - tle, Glo - ry be to you!
5. Sing your praise to God our Fa - ther, Glo - ry be to you!

All

1. LI - VING GOD, WE COME BE – FORE YOU, GLO – RY BE TO YOU!
2. GOD OF TRUTH, OUR DOUBTS DIS - PEL - LING, GLO - RY BE TO YOU!
3. FAITH - FUL GOD WHO KEEPS HIS PRO - MISE, GLO - RY BE TO YOU!
4. GOD OF PEACE, YOU HEAL OUR SAD - NESS, GLO - RY BE TO YOU!
5. PRAISE THE SON AND HO - LY SPI - RIT, GLO - RY BE TO YOU!

Cantor

1. Hosts of heav'n, your prai - ses are sing - ing. Shouts of joy and thanks are ring - ing.
2. Light of God on all men daw - ning, Christ the ri - sing sun brings mor - ning.
3. As your church, we ga - ther be-fore you, And with thanks, we sing and a - dore you.
4. Called by you, we ha - sten to meet you, And to - ge - ther pray as we greet you.
5. Ab - ba Fa - ther, Lord of cre - a - tion, Je - sus Lord, who brought sal - va - tion.

All

1. WE ON EARTH RE - ECH– O THEIR PRAI –SES: GLO - RY BE TO YOU!
2. YOU HAVE SHED YOUR LIGHT ON OUR PATH-WAY, GLO - RY BE TO YOU!
3. NOW MADE ONE IN CHRIST LET US PRAISE YOU, GLO - RY BE TO YOU!
4. WITH YOUR LO - VING KIND-NESS SUR-ROUND US, GLO - RY BE TO YOU!
5. HO - LY SPI - RIT DWEL-LING WITH-IN US, GLO - RY BE TO YOU!

112

HOLY MARY FULL OF GRACE

Michael Hodgetts

Paul Décha

1. When cre - a - tion was— be - gun, God had cho - sen you to
2. When cre - a - tion was— re - stored, You were there be - side the
3. You are with us day— by day, In our joys and our dis -
4. Lead us to your child— a - bove: He will teach us how to
5. In the vi - sion which_ trans - cends All our dreams and ne - ver
6. Praise the Fa - ther and— the Son, And the Spi - rit, three in

1. be Mo - ther of his bles - sed Son, Ho - ly Ma - ry full— of grace.
2. Lord, whom you che - rished and_ a - dored, Ho - ly Ma - ry full— of grace.
3. may. Make us joy - ful as— we say, 'Ho - ly Ma - ry full— of grace'.
4. love, How to pi - ty and_ for - give, Ho - ly Ma - ry full— of grace.
5. ends, God will ga - ther all— his friends In the King - dom of— your Son.
6. one, As it was when time_ be - gan Now and e - ver - more._ A - men.

Refrain

A - ve, A - ve, A - ve Ma - ri - a.

THIS IS MY WILL

James Quinn
based on Jn 15

Gaelic

1. This is my will,— my one com - mand,— That love should
2. No grea - ter love,— a man can have,— Than that he
3. I call you now,— no lon - ger slaves; — No slave knows
4. You chose not me, — but I chose you,— That you should
5. All that you ask — my Fa - ther dear— For my name's

1. dwell — a - mong you all._ This is my will,— that_ you should
2. die_ to save his friends,— You are my friends, if_ you o -
3. all — his mas - ter does. — I call you friends, for_ all I
4. go — and bear much fruit._ I chose you out — that_ you in
5. sake — you shall re - ceive._ This is my will,— my— one com -

1. love As I have shown— that I love you._
2. bey_ What I com - mand— that you should do. —
3. hear_ My Fa - ther say, — you hear from me. —
4. me_ Should bear much fruit — that will a - bide. —
5. mand,_ That love should dwell — in each, in all. —

113

LOVE IS HIS WORD

Luke Connaughton

Anthony Milner

1. Love is his word, love is his way, Feas - ting with men, Fas - ting a - lone,
2. Love is his way, love is his mark, Sha - ring his last Pass - o - ver feast,
3. Love is his mark, love is his sign, Bread for our strength, wine for our joy,
4. Love is his sign, love is his news, 'Do this', he said, 'lest you for - get
5. Love is his news, love is his name, We are his own, chosen and cal - led,
6. Love is his name, love is his law, Hear his com-mand, all who are his:
7. Love is his law, love is his word: Love of the Lord, Fa - ther and Word,

1. Li - ving and dy - ing, ri - sing a - gain, Love, on- ly love, is his way.
2. Christ at his ta - ble, host to the twelve, Love, on- ly love, is his mark.
3. 'This is my bo - dy, this is my blood', Love, on- ly love, is his sign.
4. all my deep sor - row, all my dear blood', Love, on- ly love, is his news.
5. Fa - mi - ly, breth - ren, cou - sins and kin. Love, on- ly love, is his name.
6. 'Love one a - no - ther, I have loved you' Love, on- ly love, is his law.
7. Love of the Spi - rit, God, eve - ry one, Love, on- ly love, is his word.

Refrain

Ri - cher than gold is the love of my Lord: Bet - ter than splen- dour and wealth.

LUMEN CHRISTI! ALLELUIA! AMEN!

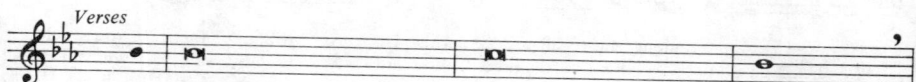

Jn 8:12, Mt 5.14, I Pet 2.9

Jean Paul Lécot

Refrain

Lu - men Chris - ti! Al - le - lu - ia! A - men!

Verses

1. I am the light of the world
2. You are the light of the world
3. Tell the wonderful deeds of the Lord

1. He who follows me will not walk in darkness. R.
2. Let your light shine before men. R.
3. He called you from darkness to light. R.

114

THE PRAYER OF THE CHURCH

The Divine Office belongs to the whole body of the faithful, lay people as well as priests and religious. The Church encourages the faithful to celebrate her official prayer together. In this way they learn to adore God the Father in spirit and in truth.

HYMNS FOR MORNING AND EVENING PRAYER

The hymn is intended to be "an easy and pleasant opening to the prayer" *(General Instruction 42)*. It should express the theme or characteristic of the hour being celebrated and should reflect the liturgical season. (See The Liturgical Year, page 24.)

MORNING PRAYER

Themes: consecration of the day, light, resurrection and praise (especially praise for creation).
Examples of morning hymns are:

The light of Christ 117
Priestly people (Verses 3 and 4)   64
Fill us with your praise   101
Glory of creation   88
Morning has broken   90
Day by day   91
May Christ live in our hearts   95
All of my life   71
Yahweh   94
This day God gives me   90
Glory be to you   112
Let us welcome the Lord (verses 1, 2 + 5)   105
Others may be chosen according to the above principles.

EVENING PRAYER

Themes: Thanks for the day, rest, redemption, evening sacrifice, light, Christ, the sun which never sets.
Some examples of evening hymns are:

Christ is alive   76
Christ, Our Lord (Verses 4 to 6)   81
Come to me   97
The light of Christ   117
Let all who are baptised   100
Without seeing you   67
Steadfast love   87
Yahweh (Verses 2 and 3)   94
Glory be to you   112
Lumen christi   114
Others may be chosen according to the above principles.

VESPERS

In the early Church, Christians gathered together at dusk to praise God and to thank him for the day that was drawing to a close. The setting sun and the lighting of the lamp reminded them that Christ is the light of the world, the sun that never sets.

The Church invites the whole body of the faithful, lay people as well as priests and religious, to join in the evening prayer of praise. We thank God for his gifts of today and every day, especially for the gift of Christ his son, our brother. We let our prayer rise like incense to God, and through Christ and with him we make intercession for the needs of the Church and of the world.

INTRODUCTORY VERSE

O God, come to our aid. ℞ O Lord, make haste to help us

Glory be to the Father and to the Son and to the Ho-ly Spi-rit. As it was in the beginning,

is now and e - ver shall be, world with-out end A - men. *Al - le - lu - ia.

*Omit during Lent.

HYMN

THE LIGHT OF CHRIST

Donald Fishel

Refrain
(Women)

C   F   Dm   G

The light of Christ has come in-to the world. The

(Men) The light of Christ has come in - to the world.

C   F   G   C

light of Christ has come in - to the world.

The light of Christ has come.

Verses

F   C   F   G   C

1. All men must be born a - gain to see the King-dom of God. The
2. God gave up his on - ly Son out of love for the world, so that
3. The light of God has come to us so that we might have sal - va - tion; from the

F   G   C   Am   Dm   G

1. wa - ter and the Spi - rit bring new life in God's love. ℞
2. all men who be - lieve in him will live for - e - ver. ℞
3. dark-ness of our sins we walk in - to glo - ry with Christ Je - sus. ℞

117

PSALMODY

PSALM 22

As a shepherd safely leads his sheep, so God brings his people home.

Thomas Egan

Refrain

The Lord is my Shep-herd, there is no-thing I shall want.

Verses

1. The Lord is my Shep - herd. There is nothing I shall want.
2. Near restful waters he leads me, to re - vive my droo-ping spi-rit.
3. If I should walk in the valley of dark - ness, no e - vil would I fear.
4. You have prepared a banquet for me, in the sight of my foes.
5. Surely his goodness and kindness shall fol-low me, all the days of my life.

1. Fresh and green are the pas - tures where he gives me re - pose. —
2. He guides me along the right path. He is true to his name. —
3. You are there with your crook and your staff, with these you give me com-fort.
4. My head you have anoin - ted with oil, my cup is o - ver - flo-wing.
5. In the Lord's own house shall I dwell, for e - ver and e - ver.

Other appropriate psalm verses may be sung to the above
melody with the refrain - 'The Lord is my Shepherd'.

PSALM 114

We must experience many hardships before we can enter the kingdom of God
(*Acts 14:22*). (This psalm may be recited by a solo speaker.)

I love the Lord for he has heard
The cry of my appeal;
For he turned his ear to me
In the day when I called him.

How gracious is the Lord, and just;
Our God has compassion.
The Lord protects the simple hearts;
I was helpless so he saved me.

They surrounded me, the snares of death,
With the anguish of the tomb;
They caught me, sorrow and distress,
I called on the Lord's name,
O Lord, my God, deliver me!

Turn back, my soul, to your rest
For the Lord has been good.
He has kept my soul from death,
My eyes from tears,
And my feet from stumbling.

I will walk in the presence of the Lord
In the land of the living.
Glory be. . . .

CANTICLE

SALVATION, GLORY, AND POWER

Rev 19: 1-2, 5-7

Adapted from chants of the
Byzantine Liturgy ,by
Margaret Daly

Refrain I

Al - le - lu - ia, al - le - lu - ia, Al - le - lu - ia.

Verses *Refrain II*

1. Sal - va - tion, glo - ry and power be - long to our God. Al - le - lu - ia.

His judge -ments are true and just. ℟.I

Refrain II

2. Praise our God, you his ser - vants. Al - le - lu - ia.

You who fear him, small and great. ℟.I

Refrain II

3. The Lord our God the al - migh - ty reigns. Al - le - lu - ia.

Let us re - joice and ex - ult and give him the glo - ry. ℟.I

Refrain II

4. The mar-riage of the Lamb has__ come Al - le - lu - ia.

And his bride has made her- self rea - dy. ℟.I

Refrain II

5. Praise the Fa - ther, the Son and the Spi - rit. Al - le - lu - ia.

Now and for - e - ver, A - men. ℟.I

ALTERNATIVE CANTICLE FOR LENT
CHRIST SUFFERED FOR YOU

Christ the servant of God freely accepts his passion

I Pet 2:21—24

Joseph Walshe

Antiphon

For our sake God made him to be sin who knew no sin,

so that in him we might be-come the right - eous - ness of God.

Verses

1. Christ suf-fered for you, leav - ing you an ex - am - ple that

you should fol - low in his steps. ℟ By his wounds we have been healed.

2. He com - mit - ted no sin; no guile was found on his lips. When he was re - viled, he

did not re - vile in re - turn. ℟ By his wounds we have been healed.

3. When he suf-fered, he did not threat - en; but he trust - ed in

him who judg - es just - ly. ℟ By his wounds we have been healed.

4. He him-self bore our sins in his bod-y on the tree, that we might die to sin and

live to right - eous- ness. ℟ By his wounds we have been healed.

5. For you were stray -ing like sheep, but now have re -turned to the

shep- herd and guard - ian of your souls. ℟ By his wounds we have been healed.

6. Give praise to the Fath - er al - migh-ty; to his son, Je - sus Christ the

Lord; to the Spi - rit who dwells in our hearts, both

now and for e - ver, A - men. ℟ By his wounds we have been healed.

Repeat — For our sake . . .

SCRIPTURE READING

This may be followed by a homily or a silent pause.

SONG OF MARY

THE LOURDES MAGNIFICAT

Paul Décha

Refrain I

The Lord has shown his power in me, Ho-ly is his name.

Refrain II

God. fills me with joy, Al-le-lu - ia, his ho-ly pre-sence is my robe, Al-le-lu - ia.

Verses

1. My soul now glo - ri - fy	The Lord who is my sa - viour.	Re -
2. The world shall call me blest	And pon-der on my sto - ry.	In
3. For those who are his friends	And keep his laws as ho - ly,	His
4. But by his power the great,	The proud, the self con - cci - ted,	The
5. He feeds the star-ving poor,	He guards his ho - ly na - tion,	Ful -
6. Then glo - ri - fy with me,	The Lord who is my sa - viour	One

1. - joice for who am I	That God has shown me fa - vour. ℟
2. me is man - i - fest	God's great - ness and his glo - ry. ℟
3. mer - cy ne - ver ends	And he ex - alts the low - ly. ℟
4. Kings who sit in state	Are hum - bled and de - fea - ted. ℟
5. - fil - ling what he swore	long since in re - ve - la - tion. ℟
6. Ho - ly Tri - ni - ty	For e - ver and for - e - ver. ℟

INTERCESSIONS

Through the Gospel, the Lord Jesus calls us to share in his glory.
Let us make our prayer with him to our heavenly Father.
(This response is sung after each intercession.)

℟ Lord, in your mer – cy hear our prayer

THE LORD'S PRAYER

Music setting, pages 20 and 21.

CONCLUDING PRAYER

CONCLUSION OF THE HOUR

WHEN A PRIEST OR DEACON PRESIDES

Roman missal

The Lord be with you R. And al-so with you

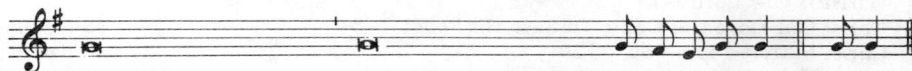

May almighty God bless you, the Father and the Son and the Ho-ly Spi-rit R A-men

Lucien Deiss

Go in the peace of Christ. R Thanks be to God.

WHEN A LAY PERSON PRESIDES

The Lord bless us, and keep us from all e-vil, and bring us to e-ver-las-ting life. R A-men.

INDEX OF PSALMS, HYMNS AND BIBLICAL SONGS

124

*Psalms marked with an asterisk are the nine psalms on the basic
national programme for Ireland.

INDEX OF FIRST LINES

INDEX OF PSALMS

Old Testament canticles are included as psalms. The nine psalms on the national programme for Ireland are marked with an asterisk.